Organisation and Management of Hotels

Organisation and Management of Hotels

By

B.K. Kochhar

2008

CYBER TECH PUBLICATIONS
4264/3, Ansari Road, Daryaganj, New Delhi-110002 (India)
Ph.: 011-23244078. Fax: 011-23280028
E-Mail: cyberpublicationsdelhi@yahoo.com

ORGANISATION AND MANAGEMENT OF HOTELS

B.K. Kochhar

First Edition 2008

Published by :

G.S. Rawat for **Cyber Tech Publications**
4264/3, Ansari Road, Daryaganj, New Delhi-110002 (India)
Ph.: 011-23244078. Fax: 011-23280028
E-Mail: cyberpublicationsdelhi@yahoo.com

Printed at : **Asian Offset Printers**

Preface

Hotel Organization and Management, helps readers to develop the wide-ranging knowledge and analytical skills they need to succeed in today's burgeoning and dynamic hotel industry. Featuring contributions from 60 leading industry professionals and academics, this comprehensive presentation encourages critical thinking by exposing readers to different viewpoints within a coherent theoretical structure, enabling them to formulate their own ideas and solutions.

Each chapter of the book examines a specific hotel department or activity and presents a variety of viewpoints on the duties, responsibilities, problems, and opportunities encountered there. Multidimensional case studies challenge readers to identify the central issues in complex management problems, understand the structure and resources of the department in question, and find solutions that may involve other hotel resources and departments. This book provides a solid introduction to every aspect of hotel management

Complete with extensive references and suggestions for further reading, Hotel Organization and Management, is an ideal book for university hospitality programs and management training programs within the hotel industry. This book helps readers develop the wide-ranging knowledge and analytical skills they need to succeed in today's burgeoning and dynamic hotel industry This comprehensive volume encourages critical thinking by providing different points of view through contributions from sixty leading industry professionals and academics. Within a coherent theoretical structure, this updated edition enables readers to formulate their own ideas and solutions.

—Author

Contents

1

The Hotel

MEANING AND DEFINITION

A hotel is an establishment that provides paid lodging, usually on a short-term basis. Hotels often provide a number of additional guest services such as a restaurant, a swimming pool or childcare. Some hotels have conference services and meeting rooms and encourage groups to hold conventions and meetings at their location.

Hotels differ from motels in that most motels have drive-up, exterior entrances to the rooms, while hotels tend to have interior entrances to the rooms, which may increase guests' safety and present a more upmarket image.

In Australia, a hotel may also be an establishment that serves alcoholic drinks, and usually meals in a casual setting but which does not necessarily provide accommodation. This type of establishment would more usually be called a pub or bar in other countries. In general use in Australia the terms '"hotel" and pub are usually taken to be synonymous.

In India, the word may also refer to a restaurant since the best restaurants were always situated next to a good hotel.

BEGINNING

The word hotel derives from the French hotel, which referred to a French version of a townhouse, not a place offering accommodation (in contemporary usage, hotel has the meaning of "hotel", and hotel particulier is used for the old meaning). The French spelling (with the circumflex) was once also used in English, but is now rare. The circumflex replaces the 's' once preceding the 't' in the earlier hostel spelling, which over time received a new, but closely related meaning.

THE SERVICES

Basic accommodation of a room with only a bed, a cupboard, a small table and a washstand has largely been replaced by rooms with en-suite bathrooms and, more commonly in the United States than elsewhere, climate control. Other features found may be a telephone, an alarm clock, a TV, and broadband Internet connectivity.

Food and drink may be supplied by a mini-bar (which often includes a small refrigerator) containing snacks and drinks (to be paid for on departure), and tea and coffee making facilities (cups, spoons, an electric kettle and sachets containing instant coffee, tea bags, sugar, and creamer or milk). In the United Kingdom a hotel is required by law to serve food and drinks to all comers within certain stated hours; to avoid this requirement it is not uncommon to come across "private hotels" which are not subject to this requirement.

However, in Japan the capsule hotel supplies minimal facilities and room space.

TYPES OF HOTELS

The cost and quality of hotels are usually indicative of the range and type of services available. Due to the enormous increase in tourism worldwide during the last decades of the 20th century, standards, especially those of smaller establishments, have improved considerably. For the sake of greater comparability, rating systems have been introduced, with the one to five stars classification being most common.

Boutique Hotels

"Boutique Hotel" is a term originating in North America to describe intimate, usually luxurious or quirky hotel environments. Boutique hotels differentiate themselves from larger chain or branded hotels by providing an exceptional and personalized level of accommodation, services and facilities.

Boutique hotels are furnished in a themed, stylish and/ or aspirational manner. Although usually considerably smaller than a mainstream hotel (ranging from 3 to 100 guest rooms) boutique hotels are generally fitted with telephone and wi-fi Internet connections, honesty bars and often cable/pay TV. Guest services are attended to by 24 hour hotel staff. Many boutique hotels have on site dining facilities, and the majority offer bars and lounges which may also be open to the general public. Of the total travel market a small percentage are discerning travellers, who place a high importance on privacy, luxury and service delivery. As this market is typically corporate travellers, the market segment is non-seasonal, high-yielding and repeat, and therefore one which boutique hotel operators target as their primary source of income.

Famous Hotels

Some hotels have gained their renown through tradition, by hosting significant events or persons, such as Schloss Cecilienhof in Potsdam, Germany, which derives its fame from the so-called Potsdam Conference of the World War II allies Winston Churchill, Harry Truman and Joseph Stalin in 1945. Other establishments have given name to a particular meal or beverage, as is the case with the Waldorf Astoria in New York City, USA, known for its Waldorf Salad or the Raffles Hotel in Singapore, where the drink Singapore Sling was invented. Another example is the Hotel Sacher in Vienna Austria, home of the Sachertorte. There are also hotels which became much more popular through films like the Grand

Hotel Europe in Saint Petersburg, Russia when James Bond stayed there in the Blockbuster, Goldeneye. Cannes hotels such as the Carlton or the Martinez become the centre of the world during Cannes Film Festival (France).

A number of hotels have entered the public consciousness through popular culture, such as the Ritz Hotel in London, UK ('Putting on The Ritz') and Hotel Chelsea in New York City, subject of a number of songs and also the scene of the alleged stabbing of Nancy Spungen by her boyfriend Sid Vicious. Hotels that enter folklore like these two are also often frequented by celebrities, as is the case both with the Ritz and the Chelsea. Other famous hotels include the Beverly Hills Hotel, the Hotel Bel-Air and the Chateau Marmont, in California, Watergate complex in Washington DC, the Hotel Astoria in Saint Petersburg, Russia, the Hotel George V and Hotel Ritz in Paris, Palazzo Versace hotel on the Gold Coast, Queensland, Australia, Hotel Hermitage and Hotel de Paris in Monaco (in the French Riviera), Peninsula Hotel in Hong Kong and Hotel Leningradskaya in Moscow.

Unusual Hotels

Many hotels can be considered destinations in themselves, by dint of unusual features of the lodging and/or its immediate environment:

Treehouse Hotels

Some hotels, such as the Costa Rica Tree House in the Gandoca-Manzanillo Wildlife Refuge, Costa Rica, or Treetops Hotel in Aberdare National Park, Kenya, are built with living trees as structural elements, making them treehouses.

The Ariau Towers near Manaus, Brazil is in the middle of the Amazon, on the Rio Negro. Bill Gates even invested and had a suite built there with satellite internet/phone.

Another hotel with treehouse units is Bayram's Tree Houses in Olympos, Turkey.

Garden Hotels

Garden hotels, famous for their gardens before they became hotels, includes Gravetye Manor, the home of William Robinson and Cliveden, designed by Charles Barry with a rose garden by Geoffrey Jellicoe.

Underwater Hotels

As of 2005, the only hotel with an underwater room that can be reached without Scuba diving is Utter Inn in Lake Mälaren, Sweden. It only has one room, however, and Jules' Undersea Lodge in Key Largo, Florida, which requires scuba diving, is not much bigger.

Hydropolis is an ambitious project to build a luxury hotel in Dubai, UAE, with 220 suites, all on the bottom of the Persian Gulf, 20 meters (66 feet) below the surface. Its architecture will feature two domes that break the surface and an underwater train tunnel, all made of transparent materials such as glass and acrylic.

Other Unusual Hotels

The Library Hotel in New York City is unique in that its ten floors are arranged according to the Dewey Decimal System.

The Rogers Centre, formerly SkyDome, in Toronto, Canada is the only stadium to have a hotel connected to it, with 70 rooms overlooking the field.

The Burj al-Arab hotel in Dubai, United Arab Emirates, built on an artificial island, is structured in the shape of a sail of a boat.

The RMS Queen Mary in Long Beach, California is the only 1930s ocean liner still in existence. Its elegant first-class staterooms are now used as a hotel. The Oriental Pearl Tower in Shanghai houses an extremely expensive hotel with only 20 rooms.

World-record Setting Hotels

Tallest

The tallest hotel in the world is the Burj al-Arab in Dubai, United Arab Emirates, at 321 metres, which however will soon be surpassed by the nearby Rose Rotana Suites at 333 meters (1,091 feet).

The Ryugyong Hotel in Pyongyang was intended to reach 330 meters (1,083 feet), but is unlikely to be completed; it has been under construction since 1987 and was abandoned in 1992. The highest hotel rooms are in the Grand Hyatt in the Jin Mao Building in Shanghai, the highest floor being at around 350 m.

Largest

The largest hotel in the world is the MGM Grand Las Vegas in Las Vegas, Nevada, USA with a total of 6,276 rooms as of December 20, 2006. On December 18, 2006 Guinness World Records listed the First World Hotel in Genting Highlands, Malaysia as the worlds largest hotel. It has a total of 6,118 rooms and is part of the Genting Highlands Resort and Casino.

The First World Plaza which is joined to the two hotel towers boasts 500,000 square feet of indoor theme park, shopping centres, casino gaming areas, and eateries. Previously, Guinness had listed the MGM Grand Las Vegas in Las Vegas, Nevada, USA with 5,005 rooms as the largest hotel in the world.

Oldest

According to the Guinness Book of World Records, the oldest hotel still in operation is the Hoshi Ryokan, in Awazu, Japan. It opened in 717, and features hot springs.

Hotel Occupations

The owner, chairman, or CEO of a hotel or hotel group is known as a hotelier.

Hotels in Fiction

Hotels have been chosen by authors as settings for crime fiction, farce and mystery works. A hotel is perfect as a mysterious, anonymous setting where various characters may gather. Hotels also feature in films, television series, songs and even theme park rides.

Cave Hotels

Desert Cave Hotel in Coober Pedy, South Australia and the Cuevas Pedro Antonio de Alarcón (named after the author) in Guadix, Spain, as well as several hotels in Cappadocia, Turkey, are notable for being built into natural cave formations, some with rooms underground.

Capsule Hotels

Capsule hotels are a type of economical hotels that are quite common in Japan.

Ice Hotels

Ice hotels, such as the Ice Hotel in Jukkasjärvi, Sweden, melt every spring and are rebuilt out of ice and snow each winter.

Snow Hotels

The Mammut Snow Hotel in Finland is located within the walls of the Kemi snow castle, which is the biggest in the world. It includes The Mammut Snow Hotel, The Castle Courtyard, The Snow Restaurant and a chapel for weddings, etc. Its furnishings and its decorations, such as sculptures, are made of snow and ice.

There is snow accommodation also in Lainio Snow Hotel in Lapland (near Ylläs), Finland.

2

Indian Management System

MEANING AND DEFINITION

Spreading over 3m square kilometres, India rises in the snowy peaks of Kashmir in the north, and falls to the tropical shores of Kerala's southern tip. In the west the barren rocky deserts of Rajasthan provide an arid, hostile environment, while in Bengal to the east lush jungles create a haven for wildlife. India's size and diversity is matched by very few countries. Dotted across this vast and breathtaking countryside are huge metropolises, swelling secondary cities and many thriving regional centres, over 40 cities with populations 1m strong, all with their own particular industries and economies. But despite India's huge scale, contrasting regions and scattered cities, one thing does link this spectacular country, growth.

The figures are staggering. India contains over 1.13 billion people, and is predicted to become the world's most populous country by 2050, overtaking China as it swells to 1.6 billion. Three cities-Mumbai, Delhi and Kolkata-contain over 10m inhabitants, and those figures rise daily. The northerly state of Uttar Pradesh has a population of over 139m-approaching the 143m living in the whole of Russia and making it the most populated internal region in the world. Likewise, India's economy is growing at speed. Real gross domestic product (GDP) grew by 8.5% in 2005, a further 8.8% in 2006, and according to the Economist Intelligence Unit (EIU) this trend will continue in 2007-08. Yes, India is on the move and the hotel industry is not being left behind. Across India average room rates are sky-rocketing. In the twelve months to March 2007 average room rates have risen 28.7% to US$174, driving revenue per available room (revPAR) up 26.9% to US$122. The Indian hotel market however, does suffer from limited supply. There arc an estimated 105,000 hotel rooms in India-a number comparable to that of Manhattan. This lack of supply, especially in the lower end of the market, combined with increased demand, is allowing hoteliers to push up average room rates.

For the first time India looks like becoming a major force in the world hotel industry. So what is fuelling this dramatic growth, and how sustainable is it? In this article we shall look at the factors defining this exciting period in India's history. To gauge these trends there are no better places to look than India's four major gateway cities-Delhi in the north, Chennai in the south, Kolkata in the east, and Mumbai in the west.

THE GREAT ECONOMY

It has to be recognised that it is not India's hotel industry alone that is prospering. Across the country industries are booming, encouraged by a strong and apparently stable economy. The government is looking east, to their heavyweight partner China and the heavily Chinese influenced Association of South-East Asian Nations (ASEAN), for trade and investment. Combine this with an increasingly close relationships with the US, already excellent ties with the UK and an, albeit partial, thaw in tensions with neighbour Pakistan, and India's global network of friends looks pretty healthy. Key areas such as IT, pharmaceuticals and telecommunications have seen rapid expansion in recent years. Many companies outsource their operations to India, benefiting from a seemingly bottomless pool of skilled labour, cheap costs and hefty government incentives.

So what effect is this economic upsurge having on the hotel industry? Well, the EIU believes that approximately 80% of foreigners coming to India are there to do business. As business travel generally generates a higher spend than leisure tourism, it is plain to see why the Indian government is keen to promote this further.

International tourism expenditure in India in 2006 was some US$8.7 billion, and is expected to rise to over US$10 billion in 2008, with the lion's share of this being generated from the hotel sector.

It is no wonder therefore, that India's government is tearing down the barriers to potential inward investment and continued growth. The central government's expenditure tax is no longer applied to hotels and services charges have been slashed.

The hotel industry is now classed as part of the country's infrastructure by the government, lowering borrowing costs. The government is also issuing new long-term tourist visas to the citizens of selected countries, including the UK, Japan, Germany, France, Switzerland and Brazil. The five-year validity of the visa sends out a clear message: encourage repeat visits from wealthy tourists.

Hotel Performance

	Occupancy (%)			Average Room Rate (US$)			RavPar (US$)		
	4/2006 to 3/2007	4/2005 to 3/206	Change %	4/2005 to 3/2007	4/2005 to 3/2006	Change %	4/2005 to 3/2007	4/2005 to 3/2006	Change %
All India	70.3	71.3	-1.4	174	135	28.7	122	96	26.9
Mumbai	75.9	73.1	3.8	202	149	35.6	153	109	40.8
Kolkata	71.3	71.3	-0.1	120	88	35.7	86	63	35.6
Delhi	74.8	79.4	-5.5	225	166	35.7	168	131	28.2
Chennai	75.2	78.3	-4.0	135	102	32.5	101	80	27.2

Source: HotelBenchmark Survey by Deloitte

THE ISLAND COUNTRY

India can almost be considered an island, and in ancient times it was. Approximately 6m years ago the Indian continental plate crashed into the Eurasian continent, an impact so severe it created the largest visible mountain range on earth-the Himalayas. With such a formidable boundary to the north and two long coastlines tapering to the southern tip-where the Bay of Bengal and the Arabian Sea meet at the Indian Ocean-India can essentially only be reached by air. The volatile border regions with Pakistan and Myanmar only serve to limit land access further. With the existing road and rail network often considered time consuming, unreliable or even unsafe, and a growing number of private low-cost airlines entering the market, domestic air travel across this vast land is also becoming increasingly popular.

Given the scale of India, air travel is a key sector. Domestic air travel throughout the country is becoming a cheaper, more feasible option with private carriers Kingfisher, Jet, Air Sahara, Indigo, Spicejet and Deccan Airways all expanding their fleets and cutting fares. In response to this, the national carriers Indian Airlines and Air India are doing likewise.

The majority of international visitors arriving in India fly into one of the four gateway cities. So how are the hotel industries in these metropolises being affected by, and reacting to, the overriding nationwide trends?

DELHI: THE CAPITAL

The gateway to the north of India, Delhi is the starting point for the majority of India's tourists. The apex of the revered Golden Triangle tourist track and capital of the ancient Mughal Empire, Delhi has enough attractions of its own to enjoy before tourists set off to Agra and Jaipur. However with thriving telecommunications, IT, banking and manufacturing industries, a key English-speaking work-force and a per-capita income more than twice the national average, Delhi is also a haven for business travel.

Delhi's relevance to the world of business is enhanced by the presence of many major multinational companies, with local government actively promoting this area as a counter to the Financial Centre of Mumbai. With the exception of the Taj Group, all hotel industry major players have based themselves here.

A dramatic 35.7% rise in the twelve months to March 2007 forced Delhi's average room rates up to an incredible US$225; the highest of all Indian cities. While occupancy levels decreased slightly to 74.8%. The main reason for this is under supply, especially in the lower end of market. As with all cities in India, the market in Delhi is dominated by 5-star and 5-star deluxe properties. Efforts are being made to solve this problem; with the local government introducing, as part of their Delhi Master Plan, a scheme intended to create a more even-spread accommodation hierarchy across the city, while also developing accessibility (road, footpaths, road bridges and parking). Another impetus for this is the fact that Delhi will host the forthcoming Commonwealth Games in 2010.

Between now and the Games, new developments in the National Capital Region (NCR-including Delhi and its suburban conurbations of Gurgaon and Noida) are set to include a 320-room Novotel, a 200-room Taj Hotel, three Starwood (the 300-room Westin New Delhi, the 97-room Westin Sohna-Gurgaon and the 220-room Sheraton New Delhi) and a 319-room Leela-Kempinski joint venture. The public sector is also playing a role with the state governments of Delhi, Haryana and Uttar Pradesh having ear-marked 75 potential NCR sites for hotel development.

Together with Mumbai, Delhi accounts for the bulk of inward arrivals. The modernisation plan for Indira Gandhi

International Airport by its new private owners is already underway. This is expected to be completed by 2010 and will more than double its capacity.

MUMBAI

The capital of the western Maharashtra state, Mumbai was created as a deep water port by the British and Portuguese, and began to boom following the construction of the Suez Canal. It is now the financial capital of India, home to the Reserve Bank of India, the National Stock Exchange and the more traditional Bombay Stock Exchange, contributing an estimated 40% of India's foreign trade. Mumbai also has thriving industries revolving around IT, engineering and healthcare sectors. Most Indian conglomerates have their corporate offices here, including Tatas, Birlas and Reliance. This status makes Mumbai a haven for national and international business travel.

Mumbai experienced revPAR growth of 40.8% in the year to March 2007. This, again, is due to a sharp increase in average room rates, which rose 35.6% to US$202 over the same period. Occupancy for this period stands at 75.9%. Once again an extremely top-heavy market dominated by luxury properties, as well as a shortfall in supply, is forcing this trend. Increased capacity at Mumbai's Chatrapati Shivaji International Airport has exacerbated the problem and allowed hoteliers to force average room rates even higher. With the proposed, further expansion and modernisation of the airport by its new owners, and with the new airport planned in the eastern suburbs of Mumbai, the city looks set for an even greater increase in arrivals. Planned developments over the next two years by Marriott, Four Seasons and Accor's 300-room Sofitel Mumbai will help.

The capital of West Bengal, Kolkata is the hub of trade into eastern India. As a traditionally socialist city, Kolkata had been unattractive to inward investment. The state government (the longest serving democratically elected communist government in the world) had long favoured trades' unions and workers' rights, and consequently the post-independence days had seen Kolkata lose out as international companies located elsewhere. However since 2000 with changed leadership, IT and manufacturing sectors are now revitalising the city. With its prime location for trade routes with China and the ASEAN countries, and direct flights to Brunei, Bangkok and Singapore, Kolkata looks set to grow and grow.

Although revPAR remains the lowest of the gateway cities, Kolkata's rate of growth is among the country's highest. An average room rate rise of 35.7% in the year to March 2007 is on a par with Delhi. Average rates for this period stand at US$120, having hit a peak of US$160 in January 2007, while RevPAR grew 35.6% to US$83.

But as the city's status as a centre of industry grows in the coming years, will supply become increasingly outstripped by demand? In the hotel sector Marriott plan to open a new 250-room Courtyard property in the city by 2009, while Hilton, with its Indian development partner DLF Ltd, also has a new opening planned in the city. It remains to be seen however, if the supply of beds in the city can reach the necessary levels for the projected visitor boom.

RESORT

Despite the 12km-long Marina Beach that defines Chennai's eastern limits, the capital of Tamil Nadu state and the gateway to south India is no beach resort, but a major industrial centre. The traditional hub of India's automobile industry is also now becoming a major IT centre, housing manufacturing plants for companies such as Dell, Nokia, Samsung and Cisco. Naturally the meetings, incentives, conference and exhibitions (MICE) tourism is a major sector, with the 2,000-capacity Chennai Conference Centre providing an excellent facility. Many of the positive effects of Bangalore (India's Silicon Valley) have also rubbed off on Chennai, with many IT outfits reportedly considering Chennai more favourably due to the infrastructure that the city offers. With revPAR growth of 27.2% for the twelve months to March 2007, Chennai follows the pattern of India's gateways cities. Average room rates, rising 32.5% to US$135, accounted for this growth, while occupancy fell slightly to 75.2%. Direct air links with many ASEAN countries and the Middle East show strong potential for further growth through MICE tourism. Leela-Kempinski plan to open the 300-room Leela Palace Kempinski Chennai by 2008, while the 253-room Hilton Chennai is set to open in December 2007. Both hotels will include significant conference facilities, including a 1,600 square metre convention centre at the Leela-Kempinski.

Average rooms rates across India's gateway cities March 2006-March 2007

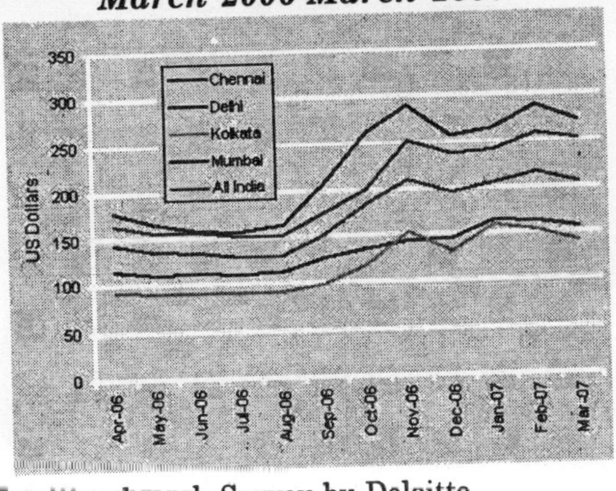

Source: HotelBenchmark Survey by Deloitte

THE AUTUMN EFFECT

The autumn time is always a good period for the Indian hotel industry. The searing temperatures of the summer months cool off to create a more visitor-friendly climate, and India's inbound tourist cycle begins. This starts in late September/early October and runs through until February or March. Inbound tourism takes a significant leap around this time, and with the government's 'Incredible India' campaign compounding the already versed impacts of India's economic growth, and increased capacity at India's two main airports in Delhi and Mumbai, 2006 was an especially good autumn. A good conference season and the fact that cricket-crazy India was hosting the autumn ICC Champions Trophy led to the number of inbound tourists growing 13% to over 4.4m in 2006.

The impact of this combination of factors saw hotels able to force room rates up dramatically. Although previous year comparisons had been positive throughout 2006, momentum gathered in autumn and October saw room rates across India rise 36% to a national average of US$196. By November this had risen further to a staggering US$215, levelling at US$205 in December. The biggest individual impact of this autumnal boom was seen in Mumbai in November 2006, when the soaring average room rates and high occupancy levels saw revPAR swell to US$213-a staggering 83% rise from the previous year.

A False Dawn

'Make hay while the sun shines', appears to be the current motto of India's hoteliers. But can average room rates be forced higher in future years and if so, how high? Already Mumbai and Delhi have average room rates comparable to the traditionally most expensive cities in Asia. Delhi's average room rate for the April 2006 to March 2007 period (US$225) outstrips all its regional rivals, including Singapore (US$138), Shanghai (US$138), Hong Kong (US$190) and Tokyo (US$196). But how high can they go?

A hotel construction boom in years to come looks like resolving the supply problem in all sectors. India's budget sector in particular looks set to take off, with Accor and Hilton planning to launch their Ibis, Formule 1 and Hilton Garden Inn brands across the country. Local operators are also expanding their portfolios, with Sarovar having launched its Hometel budget brand, and South-India based Choice Hotels looking to open 8-10 budget hotels a year in the next 3 years. And development is planned not only in the gateways cities, but new, rapidly growing metropolises such as Bangalore, Hyderabad, Pune, Chandigarh, Indore and Jaipur. Once this happens it is likely that the new competitive climate will force average room rates, even in the top end of the market, to plateau or fall.

To maintain such growth, India's economy needs to continue its boom and the government continue to invest in the country's infrastructure. There seems no reason why, with India's wealth of resources and skilled labour, the economy cannot continue to grow at speed. With a booming IT sector, India is ideally placed to thrive in the 21st century. However justification of such high average room rates can be found only in world-class facilities and back-up services for the business traveller. If the logistics of travel itself are troublesome, business people may be dissuaded from travelling to India. As India's cities attract increasing numbers of visitors, the surrounding services need to be improved.

However with the increasing supply of air travel it is becoming easy to travel around this vast, spectacular land. Whether you enter by the north, south, east or west-through Delhi, Chennai, Kolkata or Mumbai-India is now becoming more accessible. As urbanisation increases, from sprawling gateway metropolises, to the rapid-rising secondary cities, and small but swelling regional cities, the need for hotel rooms will keep pace. International chains have realised this great opportunity, and even although average room rates cannot continue to climb as steeply in future years as was seen in 2006-07, a large increase in supply will compensate for this. Growth is growth in any form.

3

THE HOSPITALITY eBUSINESS

MEANING AND DEFINITION

As hospitality industry executives contemplate the launch of the new millennium, they need to recognize the huge changes that are occurring in the way business is being conducted and begin planning in earnest as to how they will respond.

For those operating within the physical world, the concept of electronic business or "e-business" may appear to be of limited significance. But such an assumption could be costly. E-business and its applications are undoubtedly the No. 1 topic in the boardrooms of most of the world's largest companies. The financial markets are making massive investments in the companies that deliver Internet technologies, content and related products and services, and the corporate world is now moving toward e-business offerings at a rapid clip.

On the business-to-business (b-to-b) front, e-business is projected to grow enormously in the United States over the next several years, with business-to-consumer (b-to-c) trade not as big, but growing just as fast. The McKenna Group estimates that the b-to-b marketplace could grow in value to US$500 billion in 2003. But those estimates may be low. General Motors Corporation, Ford Motor Company and Daimler Chrysler, for example, have just announced that they plan to combine their efforts to form a b-to-b integrated supplier exchange through a single global portal. Meanwhile, on the retail front, the race is on to win the Internet consumer, whose ranks are growing rapidly. Traditional retailers have much to be concerned about as retail sales over the Internet skyrocket. And while such activity has yet to grow to the same extent in Europe and Asia/Pacific where the cost of phone calls remains an issue, it surely will over time. In the meantime, travel is one of the more popular online products for sale and over the next several years, it is projected in the United States alone to grow to US$12 billion.

E-business is rewriting the economic rules globally for every industry-including hospitality, travel and leisure. Indeed, it's important to recognize that we are now operating in what has been described as the "new economy," as global trends drive change, including globalization, consolidation, convergence, technology and communications. Even more, it is clear that the underlying sources of value are also changing. Use of intangible assets such as information, brands, customers, relationships and networks distinguish the most successful companies in the world.

EFFECTS OF THE INTERNET

It is clear that the Internet is having a huge impact on how we conduct our lives and our businesses. And it arrived virtually overnight. In the United States, for example, it took 38 years for television to get into 50 million homes. For the Internet, it took just five years. And for those U.S. consumers that are online, four out of five believe that the Internet is a more important invention than television. Of these same online consumers, close to six in 10 prefer e-mail to paper mail for business correspondence and over one in four check their e-mail while on vacation.

The Internet is also changing the customer relationship-undermining and redirecting customer attention to new sellers of products and services and away from their traditional relationships. And as this occurs, the traditional approaches that hospitality businesses have taken to distribution are all being affected. From reservations taken over the Internet, which are projected to more than double to 9% of volume over the next year, to the declining role of the travel agent. This occurs as so-called "infomediaries" provide information and access, and software robots troll the activity online to develop matches between buyers and sellers, analyzing complex patterns and looking for trends for marketers to capitalize upon. As for the infomediaries, we can expect some of these to move into the transactions business and continue the process of disintermediation. For some hospitality companies, it may be best to join this new competition, particularly if it cannot be beaten at its own gamc.

The reality today is that the balance of power is shifting from sellers to buyers and in so doing it makes the importance of delivering high-quality service, convenience and value for money ever more compelling. The Internet has clearly levelled the playing field by making price information broadly available to the consumer. Internet business models affect product and services offerings, pricing, distribution and customer service, as well as long-term information capabilities. As a consequence, some hospitality suppliers will inevitably feed different tranches of their inventory through the various channels at their disposal-including the Internet, travel management organizations, destination packagers and the like.

THE CONVENIENCE AND CONSISTENCY

In the end, customers want both convenience and consistency. They don't have all the leisure time that futurists once predicted they would have by now. In fact, they have less. Today's fast-paced world produces ever more stress, and consumers want information and they want it fast. And if hospitality companies and travel providers don't deliver convenience, somebody else inevitably will. They also want to be wired up to the rest of the world-at home, in their office and especially when they travel. And for hoteliers trying to cope with in-room technologies and the delivery of high-speed Internet access, we will soon be seeing more integration of network communication and entertainment products to further complicate or liberate our lives, depending on your point of view.

Customers are also looking for consistency-a simple concept, but central to whether a brand has value or not. And in the emerging networked world, aligning the value propositions of alliance partners and ensuring a seamless and consistent experience will only be as good as the weakest link in the chain.

NEW BUSINESS RULES

Within this new economy, the operating environment for hospitality companies is changing. There are new rules of conduct, new relationships and new criteria for success, along with a new set of metrics. The revolution that we must now confront is therefore no less significant than the one that our forebears had to deal with as the Industrial Revolution changed how people lived, worked and dealt with each other. And like our distant relatives of centuries ago, there are boundless opportunities and countless risks, most obscured within an environment of great uncertainty. In such an era there are certain traits to business behavior that will distinguish success from failure. At this stage in the new economy's evolution, these traits would appear to include speed, agility and flexibility.

Speed is necessary to get to market early with a first-mover advantage that assures early adoption by an increasingly fickle, restless and frequently disloyal customer. Such speed is imperative as so-called "start-up" companies come to dominate their chosen niche in extremely short periods of time, frequently preempting the opportunity for those too slow to react.

Agility is required to be able to respond to competitive threats by not only those we know and can monitor, but also unseen competitors. These latter competitors may not even exist as yet, but as they emerge, they may quickly disintermediate established customer relationships.

And, finally, flexibility is needed to reorganize the established models of business and all of the related processes, and adapt the organization in organic fashion to a new environment in whatever form it takes.

PLACE TO SPACE FACTOR

For business executives at large, one of the most compelling changes that has confronted them in recent years is the potential for e-business. But while the significance of these new media are all too apparent, the business solutions required to capitalize on opportunities they offer are unfortunately not. For most hospitality executives, the essential frame of reference has been a geocentric one where real estate and geography have been the big drivers in a physical world-buildings, dots on maps, markets served, chains. In tomorrow's world, these concepts will require some fundamental adjustments to provide for market "spaces" rather than "places" as the nature of relationships between hotel businesses, their customers, their suppliers and their alliance partners go through rapid and constant change.

As these changes occur, the new economy's business leaders must quickly learn the new rules of the game and adjust their approaches accordingly. And the most successful among us will align key processes around the Internet, build corporate intelligence automatically, create integrated value chains and develop new processes to deal with an ever-changing set of circumstances.

PERSONNEL MANAGEMENT

Supporting the changes in the new economy will be a vast pool of talented human capital anxious to bring new ideas and new technologies to bear on the traditional ways of doing business and, in doing so, steadily increase the pace of productivity improvement. And if the hospitality industry is to respond to this coming reality, it will need to address some of its most vexing challenges-particularly those relating to the recruitment, training and development of human capital. The human capital inventory for an e-business will require entrepreneurship, as well as visionary leadership, strength in sales and marketing and commitment to customer relationship management. The organizational bias will need to be toward creativity and risk-taking, and away from dependency on analysis and procedures.

In addition to the human capital challenge, many of today's legacy organizations are better structured to work in the old economy, but are considerably less aligned for many activities in the "new." The cultural challenges may in fact be no less daunting than those presented by some of the technological ones. For large organizations attempting a major shift in orientation, the presence of a significant culture may turn out to be quite a hindrance.

REDEFINING HOSPITALITY BUSINESS

In some industries, profits are made on spare parts and maintenance rather than on mainstream products. In the new economy, we may see this business model replicated in the hospitality industry. And for those companies that discount or give away products such as hotel rooms in order to sell linked services, they surely will be redefining the meaning of hospitality. They will also be marketing an array of hospitality and leisure products and services to a customer base that is no longer satisfied with the traditional ways of making such purchases.

Hospitality businesses that traditionally provided room, board, management and marketing may need to rethink their roles in the new economy, particularly as services become more valuable than products. With the rapid growth of "infomediaries" and their facilitation of transactions, hospitality businesses may need to redefine themselves in order to prosper in an increasingly electronic world where one-to-one customization is the order of the day. But for those contemplating repositioning their companies in an e-business environment, it will be necessary to focus on the current value proposition of the business and determine how it might be reformatted or enhanced to ensure success in the new setting.

PREPARATION

But just how prepared is the global hospitality industry to capitalize on some of the opportunities afforded by the emerging new economy? In Arthur Andersen's recently published global survey of technology, Hospitality 2000: The Technology, we addressed some of the issues that the industry is facing. These included the closed nature of our technology architectures, the way in which we collect information on our customers, our investments in Internet, intranet and extranet technologies, and our adoption of electronic commerce. The results are not especially encouraging and suggest an industry still relatively slow to adapt to e-business. Only 39% of the industry's Web sites, for example, can handle reservations on a real-time basis, and even fewer still (19%), collect customer information. At the same time, just 22% are using "push" marketing programs and a distinct minority (just 19%), have extranets to suppliers or customers. But these adoption rates are nonetheless projected to grow and we should, therefore, expect our industry's leaders to be far more attuned to the needs of an e-business environment in the years to come.

As information technology (IT) is used to facilitate a company's entry into the world of electronic commerce, our industry's leadership will also need to overcome a natural tendency to be disappointed by the role of IT in achieving competitive advantage. For many years IT was seen as a mechanism to support back office finance and accounting functions. In the future, it inevitably will be one of the principal drivers of value creation in the new economy. But we should not be mislead by IT-in e-business, it will be the strategy, not the technology that will make the difference between success and failure. But having the strategy in place is only the first step. It must be linked to every part of the business.

E-BUSINESS PLANNING

With the costs of playing in the e-business world escalating rapidly, hospitality executives should consider the four phases of what might be called the "E-Business Lifecycle." The first of these-E-Business Strategy Development and Planning-must address the market and competitive context, articulate the vision and opportunity, outline the strategy and the business case, and identify the risks. In recent years, we have frequently seen hospitality businesses put up a Web site on the Internet and consider this an e-business strategy. But without a strategy for this new form of commerce and the business planning process to drive it, such reactionary approaches stand little chance for success. Once the plan is in place, an e-business design phase can commence to address site design, lay out the business architecture, identify the technical infrastructure, plan for performance, availability and capacity, and deal with tax issues and enterprise security.

Following the design phase, E-Business implementation will prepare for the launch with training and change enablement, implementation and integration, testing and roll-out. Once in place, E-Business Operations will need to be supported by IT and audit services, Web site activity analysis and Web site maintenance. Finally, measurement systems will need to be established to monitor performance.

As industry executives embark on this e-business lifecycle, they will need in the first stage to clearly establish the business case for investing in new technologies, systems and organizations by addressing both the cost reduction and revenue enhancement benefits. On the revenue side, there are a number of factors to consider. These include the company's ability to identify and recruit the most valuable customers; the ability to seamlessly cross-sell the company's products and services, as well as those of alliance partners; the ability to retain valuable customers and reduce attrition (especially relevant in a world of questionable brand loyalty); and finally, when and how to eliminate costly and unnecessary discounts through revenue optimization.

In this kind of environment, the property management system will no longer hold sway as the centre of the hospitality universe, but will become just one in a series of customer touch-points that will increasingly include the Internet. These touch-points will ultimately need to be fully integrated into a customer information system supported by sophisticated data warehousing and data mining technologies.

Adding to the industry's costs in this portrait of the future is the cost of grafting e-business technologies onto the industry's legacy systems. At a certain stage, it may make sense to start from scratch and ensure that every system is Web-enabled. This would allow a total interface for a high-growth e-business, thereby maximizing the customer relationship management opportunities that it presents.

SUCCESS ON THROUGH INTERNET

As to the role of the Internet, its comprehensive reach and ubiquitous nature has already ensured its central place in the new economy. But how should we evaluate whether an Internet application is deserving of our attention? Firstly, productivity on the Internet in the years to come will be vastly improved by much higher bandwidth than is currently in place. And with higher bandwidth will come applications that can benefit from such extra capacity delivering tightly focused and reliable content to an increasingly sophisticated and demanding e-customer. If an Internet application is to succeed in the future, it will therefore need to be designed to capitalize on this coming reality.

Secondly, an Internet application needs to form a community of some sort because without a sense of place, albeit of the virtual sort participants will not have that all-important sense of belonging. And as with the industrial revolution, which drew a disparate population to centers of economic activity, so will such "intranet communities" grow in value as their populations increase in size and their economic product expands. For larger businesses that form such communities, they are developing new revenue sources and are reinventing their relationships with customers, employees, suppliers and partners. Smaller companies intent on participating in this new environment, may need to be content as a participant in an established community, rather than trying to take on the creation of a community itself. It is better, perhaps, to be one of many players in a successful space than struggling to establish an identity in a world surrounded by also-rans.

Whether large or small, community developers and marketers of the virtual sort will have to recognize that what may have appeared cool in the physical world to generations brought up in the old economy will not work in the world of e-business. Being cool and staying that way in order to get and keep attention will remain a constant challenge, especially for those keen to nurture a younger generation of travellers brought up on MTV and the Web.

Finally, the successful Internet application needs to improve service while reducing transaction costs, particularly as the balance of power in the buy/sell relationship continues its inexorable migration from sellers to buyers. Service improvement strategies will be nothing new for hospitality businesses, but it is noteworthy that service (rather than on-time delivery, price or other concerns) is the top factor that encourages return e-business. This must be an area of focus since the current growth of e-business appears destined to outpace the supporting infrastructure and its related service at least over the short term. But as hospitality executives know, delivering good service can be expensive. Scaling the types of service response to the circumstances is a growing need, but one that can be modulated if the value of each customer can be distinguished and the response adjusted accordingly.

In considering the opportunities in hospitality e-business, industry leaders should take stock of the dynamics that are occurring in the new economy and plan accordingly. It is probably easy to dismiss the e-business world as a playground for others with products and services that are more obviously applicable. But our industry is changing, as is the world around us. And as alliance partners, vendors, customers, employees and systems all become Web-enabled, hospitality companies must adjust their strategies, organizations, processes and technologies accordingly.

BOTTOM LINE RULES

The demand for extended-stay lodging has existed since travellers with a little money in their pocket have had both the time and the inclination to spend time away from homes and businesses. The extended-stay concept dates back to 19th century England when visitors arrived at rooming houses in horse-drawn carriages, and travel was a more leisurely affair than it is today. Today, the extended-stay lodging sector offers diverse products that vary widely throughout the world to serve the needs of modern leisure and business travellers. And while product offerings differ on the two sides of the Atlantic, there is some consensus on the definition of extended stay. This hotel sector in a variety of forms is made up of commercially run lodging properties with suites or apartments comprising one or more rooms.

As the hospitality industry enters the 21st century, extended stay represents a significant opportunity for hotel companies, developers and investors. Interest in extended stay has been spurred by high net income margins and occupancy rates that typically surpass hotel industry averages. Indeed, extended-stay lodging can be seen as a "win-win" situation for the hotel owner and investors. Higher occupancy rates, lower construction costs and shorter periods of stabilization paint an attractive picture for hoteliers in Europe and the United States. In London, for example, occupancy levels for extended-stay properties are actually better than the already strong levels posted by conventional hotels. In the United States, extended stay was reinvented as a commercial enterprise when Marriott opened its first Residence Inn in 1974. Now, the economics of the extended-stay sector have made it a magnet for real estate investment trusts (REITs) and other investment groups in hospitality.

This article draws a profile of the extended-stay lodging sector as it has evolved in the United States and Europe, with the focus on its current state of development and economic opportunity in the future.

EXTENDED STAY

Extended-stay properties operate under several banners, but generally fall into one of three categories:

- all-suite hotels;
- apartment hotels or aparthotels; and
- serviced apartments.

The traditions and definitions of extended-stay lodging, however, differ from country to country. All-suite hotels, featuring the full range of services available at a first-class hotel in the United States, are typically not considered a part of extended-stay lodging in Europe. The apartment hotel (or aparthotel) is primarily a European term. They are popular with tourists in resort areas. Serviced apartments, which are known as corporate housing in the United States, are described as boarding houses in Germany. In Eastern European cities, the term also identifies single apartments found in various buildings that are marketed and serviced by an operator.

The lexicon of extended stay in its many variations can be attributed in part to its history of development. In the United States, extended-stay lodging has been adopted by the hotel industry as an extension of hotel lodging. Hotel companies such as Marriott have begun to penetrate the corporate housing sector with extended-stay properties for business use. As extended stay was reinvented as an extension of the hotel industry, it has continued to be identified as a complementary commercial enterprise annexed to U.S. hotel development. In contrast, the sector in Europe has grown as a separate business concept, particularly in Great Britain and France. And in Germany, the segment emerged as a product diversification among real estate developers in the early 1990s when hotels and housing were not too attractive to investors, but the combination of the two seemed to hold a potential for good returns.

Varying definitions of extended-stay lodging in Europe and the United States are also reflected in the type and volume of performance data available. In the United States, data has been developed on this segment of the hospitality industry. In Europe, however, the prevalence of serviced apartments with widely varying sites, locations and contract terms, as well as the limited supply of apartment hotels and the small markets in some cities, make it hard to obtain performance statistics and even harder to compare cities or countries from market to market.

Location

The development patterns of extended stay are also distinctly different in U.S. and European markets. European serviced apartments have traditionally been located in city centers with strong, all-season tourist and business demand. Catering mostly to leisure travellers, apartment hotels were initially unbranded. The easy availability of transportation was of primary concern. Establishing extended-stay lodging in major cities meant that many properties were converted, rather than purpose-built, offering fewer and smaller units than comparable properties in the United States. The major European aparthotel brands, Orion and Citadines, began to expand domestically in France in the late 1980s, and internationally in the early 1990s when they opened properties in Belgium, Spain, Portugal and the United Kingdom. In many cases, the bulk of supply is in the capital cities. In the United States, however, preferred extended-stay product locations are often suburban areas, usually close to suburban office parks, hospitals or senior residence communities. Southern locations fare better, mainly due to the high volume of relocation, both by companies and their employees, and by senior citizens. Although used by leisure guests, most extended-stay accommodation is located so as to be convenient to business travellers. Moreover, it has taken U.S. operators much longer to build up the domestic market and move to international locations than their European counterparts.

The difference in location types between the United States and Europe relates to the varying patterns of settlement and the level of dependence on cars. The general preference for urban locations in Europe has important implications for the economics of the projects, since land prices will typically be much higher in central areas and available plots tend to be smaller. In general, the downtown locations have meant conversions and nontraditional solutions to space and configuration problems, rather than new construction.

The greatly varying development patterns and economics in the United States and Europe will, undoubtedly, continue to translate into varying risks and rewards for developers of extended stay properties.

The U.S. extended-stay market, the world's most developed, is primarily comprised of three extended-stay products: (1) all-suite hotels; (2) limited-service hotels, and

(3) serviced apartments, the corporate housing market. The all-suite hotel is relatively common in metropolitan areas and refers to full-service hotels with two-room units, usually with a bedroom and living room. These hotels have limited public areas and services.

The apartment hotel, as its name implies, is equipped with a kitchen or kitchenette and may have one or two rooms. These hotels are often in the budget or economy class. They are typically described under the limited-service concept because they usually have fewer staff on site with food and beverage limited to a breakfast room, and they do not report food and beverage revenue. Serviced apartments-intended for the corporate housing market-are generally considered separate from the extended-stay lodging sector. Properties in this category vary widely in size, even in the same location. They have fully equipped kitchens and service is limited to daytime reception and weekly or biweekly cleaning. Typically there are no public areas such as lounges and breakfast rooms.

Supply. In the United States, there is a clear segmentation of extended-stay products among upper-, mid-and lower-tier properties, based on servicing and pricing. The pioneers in extended stay developed first-class properties. But with the increased mobility of middle-class travellers, the volume of business travel and the entry of franchise companies into the market, new brands and operators have emerged in the lower price/service tiers. The largest U.S. extended-stay hotel operators, such as Marriott and Extended-Stay America (ESA), commonly have multiple brands in each segment. In 1998, the extended-stay supply in the United States comprised 137,500 units. Of those units:

- Thirty-nine percent were in the upper tier; Marriott Residence Inn dominated that market with 303 properties.
- Twenty-nine percent fell into the mid-tier with ESA's Studio Plus at the top with 86 properties.

- Thirty-seven fell into the lower tier, with ESA leading with 222 properties.

A short history of extended-stay in the United States offers insights into the market's expansion with mid-and lower-tier properties leading in that growth. According to Smith Travel Research, upscale room supply increased by 75% between 1994 and 1998, compared to 600% for lower-category stock. The growth trend continued in 1999: by mid-year there were 179,300 rooms in extended stay properties, a 25% increase over mid-1998. Of the 30,300 rooms in the pipeline in late 1999, 37% were in the budget and economy segment, and 31% in the mid-price segment. Analysts estimate total extended-stay supply to increase to 300,000-320,000 rooms by the end of 2002, or 8% of projected hotel room supply.

Growth has been especially rapid during the last two or three years in areas with high population growth, technology industries and rapid rates of immigration. As a result, extended-stay lodging comprises up to 13% of total rooms supply in some southern cities and 9% in metropolitan centers, in contrast to only 3% of total lodging supply on a national basis.

The economics of success. Analysts expect the supply of extended-stay products to continue to grow by some 40,000 to 50,000 units per year until 2003. The interest in the sector is spurred by high net income margins and occupancy rates that typically surpass hotel industry averages. In 1998, extended-stay upper-and lower-tier properties achieved 78% and 67% occupancy, respectively. This stands in sharp contrast to the industry as a whole, which averaged 64% occupancy.

Major players that once dominated the extended-stay market are being joined by REITs and franchise companies, which have been lured by the attraction of the bottom line. Higher occupancy rates, lower construction costs and shorter periods of stabilization have caught the eye of these new entrants. Construction costs are lower because no money is spent on common area design and construction, plus the initial land costs are lower. The stabilization period tends to be shorter than hotels of comparable quality because of lower operational costs, reduced payroll, and the elimination of low-profit centers such as restaurants. Net operating income (NOI) margins of 50% are not uncommon.

FEW MORE PLAYERS

High mobility in the U.S. business sector has created a strong corporate housing market. Oakwood Corporate Housing, founded in 1969, is the world's largest serviced apartment agent and operator with more than 20,000 units in the United States, Thailand, the Philippines, China, and Britain. Large U.S. agents include CRS Corporate Housing, Preferred Living, Apartment Connection, and Corporate Housing Connection. On the Internet, two major search directories for U.S cities are now provided by Rent Net and Showcase Suites.

Some U.S.-based agents market properties worldwide. The largest are BridgeStreet Accommodations (4,000 units in the United States, Canada, Britain, France), Barclay International Group (Europe, the United States, Mexico, Israel) and Global Home Network (London, Paris, Prague).

HISTORY OF THE CONCEPT

The extended-stay concept dates back to 19th century England and a more leisurely approach to travel than today. Now, this diverse sector primarily caters to the corporate executive needing a suite or apartment with one or more rooms.

Great Britain's Market Thriving

In the United Kingdom, serviced apartments are the most common extended-stay product, but aparthotels are increasing in number. Initially the units were designed for the corporate executive or the affluent traveller, but a growing number of mid-level properties have become available during the past few years.

Supply. London represents the most highly developed corporate market in the United Kingdom, as well as Europe at large. Extended-stay supply includes 54% high-end accommodation, while 46% are mid-level properties, which are overwhelmingly located in the West End areas of Mayfair, Kensington and Knightsbridge. The aparthotel market is primarily identified by two brands: Orion and Citadines, both part of Westmont Hospitality. The largest serviced-apartment players are Park Lane Apartments with nine properties and the Cheval Group with four properties. As chain operators enter the market, consolidation and attention to branding may be expected.

Market segmentation in the United Kingdom is not based on price, as is often the case in the United States, but rather more on the size and services required by the predominant group of guests. For instance, there are properties that cater specifically to guests from the Middle East who spend the summer in London with their families and prefer finely appointed apartments with multiple bedrooms.

Extended Stay in London

London	*Units*	*Properties*
Apartment Hotels	300	4
Serviced Apartments		
High-end	1,600	44
Mid-level	1,100	12
Total	3,000	60

Source: Arthur andersen estimates.

The economics of success. Extended-stay occupancy levels in the United Kingdom are typically between 80% and 90%. As in the United States, those levels are somewhat higher than the already strong occupancy levels of hotels in London. Serviced apartments have prospered because of stable tourist and business demand for the product. The high quality of furnishings and spaciousness of the apartments have resulted in high rental rates. Hotels have also recognized the increasing market interest in serviced apartments and several have converted rooms into apartments for extended-stay use. Additionally, operational and marketing synergies make the construction of serviced apartments adjacent to a hotel good strategy.

Marketing. U.K.-based agents, such as Foxtons typically have international operations. The locations covered vary in scope from just a few properties in European capitals (Holiday Serviced Apartments) to offerings around the globe through partner affiliations (The Apartment Service). Some agents, however, are still concentrating on the domestic market and have only limited international offers (Regency Apartments).

CANADA'S HOSPITALITY SECTOR

Canada marks the millennium with celebrations spanning the country, from the Atlantic coast to the Pacific islands of British Columbia. In fact, the Millennium Foundation of Canada was the world's first organization dedicated to creating legacies to mark the year 2000.

Moreover, Canada's hospitality sector is enjoying a strong run up to the millennium, with solid occupancy rates and a robust domestic economy-a 3.3% annual growth rate-fuelling business travel.

With the Canadian dollar hovering about US$0.67 for most of the past two years, Americans and other international travellers have discovered that Canada is a great bargain. Domestic travellers, whose spending power abroad has been significantly diminished, agree.

The result has been healthy occupancy rates in the lodging industry in many major markets across the country. In

Toronto, for instance, average annual occupancy has reached a 75%, and tourist and convention spending was more than C$6.4 billion during the past year.

These positive fundamentals have not been lost on the major industry players, who through the driving force of consolidation are beginning to dominate Canada's hospitality market. During the last year, Canadian Pacific, Westmont Corp., Intrawest and others have made significant moves in their attempts to lead their industry sectors:

Canadian Pacific: In May 1998, Canadian Pacific acquired Delta Hotels, which managed or franchised approximately 10,000 rooms at 34 properties. In the deal, Canadian Pacific Hotels acquired the management company and the Delta brand, as well as leasehold interests in three properties for C$93 million. This was followed in late 1998 with the acquisition of the seven warm weather resorts of Princess Hotels from Lonrho Plc for US$540 million.

Canadian Pacific then entered into an agreement with Fairmont Hotel Management LP, creating a new hotel management company called Fairmont Hotels and Resorts Inc. This new company will manage 69 hotels, including trophy assets such as The Plaza Hotel in New York, The Fairmont in San Francisco, and The Fairmont Copley Plaza in Boston. Canadian Pacific also continues to add prestigious domestic properties to its portfolio. These include a purchase and renovation of Le Manoir Richelieu in June 1999, which recently re-opened, as well as a new Fairmont Vancouver Airport Place, which opened in October 1999.

Based in Toronto, Canadian Pacific is Canada's largest owner-operator of full service hotels, with approximately 26,000 rooms at 69 properties and 21,500 employees across Canada, the U.S., Mexico, Bermuda, Barbados and Asia.

Westmont Corp.: Industry consolidation continued into the spring of 1999, when UniHost Corp. was acquired by Westmont Corp. At the time, UniHost had the second largest multi-brand hotel operation in Canada and was among the top 10 globally, with a portfolio of 12,000 rooms at 122 properties–102 owned and the balance managed. This would be added to Westmont's existing portfolio of 8,500 rooms at 45 properties across Canada. The group now manages a wide variety of brands, including Comfort, Crowne Plaza, Holiday Inn, Holiday Inn Select, Marriott and Quality.

Westmont Corp. is operated in partnership between the Westmont Hospitality Group, which owns and operates more than 300 hotels in Canada, the U.S. and Europe, and Whitehall Street Real Estate Funds, which is managed by Goldman, Sachs & Co., New York.

Intrawest Corp.: In mid-1999, Vancouver-based Intrawest Corp., the owner of 10 mountain resorts, including Mammoth and Squaw Valley in the U.S. and the Whistler/ Blackcomb all-season resort in British Columbia, purchased 50% of Blue Mountain Resorts Ltd., the largest mountain resort in Ontario. In other skiing niche-related news, ClubCorp Resorts, the world's largest owner and operator of private clubs and golf resorts, sold Mont-Sainte-Anne, a ski resort just north of Quebec City, to Resorts of the Canadian Rockies.

Other major deals would soon follow. In June 1999, Canadian Hotel Income Properties (CHIP), a real estate investment trust (REIT), received an hostile takeover bid from another REIT, Royal Host, which has an asset base of C$300 million, which includes 3,500 rooms at 33 hotels. CHIP, Canada's first hotel REIT, owns and operates nearly 8,000 rooms at 36 hotels across Canada. Participating with Royal Host in its bid is Westmont Corp., which stands to gain a few more hotels for its new Canadian operations.

Meanwhile, activity also is occurring in other niche sectors of Canada's hospitality industry. In mid-1998, Canada's Vinings Franchise Systems and Atlanta-based U.S. Franchise Systems, reached an agreement to bring the Microtel brand concept to Canada. Microtel Inns & Suites is a growing, franchised chain of newly constructed budget and economy hotels.

Continuing this trend to bring quality budget lodging to Canada, Cendant Corp.'s Knights Franchise Systems, Inc. signed its first international master franchise agreement for the development of Knights Inn brand hotels in Canada with AFM Hospitality of Toronto. AFM, which already holds the master franchise for Cendant's Ramada and Howard Johnson brands in Canada, expects to add more than 100 Knights Inns during the next five years, recently opening its first in Niagara Falls, Ontario. AFM also recently signed a deal with Seattle-based AST Brands LLC to bring the Aston brand to Canada.

Largely attributed to Canadian "snowbirds" escaping the winter for a warm-weather holiday in the U.S. or Caribbean, Canada has long suffered a tourism trade deficit. But with tourism spending growth rate within Canada expected to top 4% annually coupled with a declining rate of growth in tourism spending by Canadians abroad, a trade balance is projected within two to three years.

Indeed, this new strength in the hospitality sector has not been lost on the industry's major players in Canada, where consolidation is not only the major trend in the industry, but also the driving force behind change as we enter the new millennium.

COMPUTERIZATION AND INFORMATION RISKS

Hotel managers awakened in the early morning hours to news of an earthquake, fire or explosion are unlikely to think first of saving the hotel's AS400 information system or retrieving computer data tapes from off-site locations. Evacuating guests and employees is paramount. Disaster plans put people first. Nevertheless, loss of a property's information technology (IT) functions can plunge any company into operational disarray, triggering revenue losses and negative publicity that may take years to overcome. Technology systems rendered inoperable in one location can ripple through an entire hotel organization, forcing the company to fall back on manual operations. Reservations, property management and communications systems must be quickly replaced and guest data recovered to avoid major losses.

A case in point involved the bombing of New York's World Trade Centre in 1993. The terrorist act inflicted physical damage to a large area of downtown Manhattan, including an adjacent hotel. Although the hotel was evacuated in less than fifteen minutes with no fatalities, the telephone and computer system was damaged. The hotel could not account for guests and employees. Communications failures prevented management from communicating with emergency services. The loss of heat could have caused further damage to existing systems from the bursting of frozen water pipes. The hotel's experience points to one of the key elements in a technology disaster recovery plan-maintaining critical operational and financial data at an off-site storage facility. Following a disaster, off-site facilities that maintain reservation and accounting information would be available immediately for retrieval of in-house guest records, financial documents, guest history and sales information, minimizing a disaster's effect on a hotel's data and information.

Prompted by insurance companies or experience, most companies have addressed the need for a disaster recovery plan (DRP), if not put one in place. Few, however, create and maintain written plans on IT disaster recovery. In a survey conducted by Comdisco, Inc., one of the largest disaster recovery companies, it was estimated that only 45 percent of companies maintain a formal plan in the event of computer disruption.

The survey addressed the level of corporate readiness for disaster recovery, concluding that only 12 percent of enterprises have an effective disaster recovery plan. Another 6 percent were partially prepared. Fully 82 percent of companies were ineffectively prepared for a technology disaster. The survey measured: 1) data centers, 2) local area networks, and 3) enterprise wide area networks. While the survey itself was cross-industry, hospitality companies rely heavily on all three of the technology components measured. A disaster recovery plan specifically addressing technology is essential to any hotel's risk management programs.

Technology Systems Harms

One of the most destructive events for hospitality companies occurred in September 1992 as Hurricane Iniki unleashed winds up to 200 miles per hour on the Island of Kauai, Hawaii. The damage amounted to $1.6 billion and resulted in 85 percent of the island's hotel rooms shutting down for at least two months. With 30-foot waves and complete power outages, all hotel technology systems on the island were lost.

Particularly in areas with potential for destructive weather, the need for disaster recovery and off-site back up systems cannot be overstated. Hotel properties without technology disaster recovery plans may be closed for much longer periods of time than other companies.

Of the 320 technology recoveries supported by Comdisco since 1985, hardware failure was the largest cause at 24 percent, followed by hurricanes and power outages at 16 percent each, and floods accounting for another 15 percent. The seeds of major technology failures may occur within the systems themselves. One of the largest providers of global distribution of airline and hotel reservations experienced an outage in mid-1998 due to a software error, resulting in the complete cessation of new reservations bookings for more than five hours. An outage on a system that processes an hourly average of 45,000 airline and hotel reservations can cause major service disruptions and customer dissatisfaction.

Even a supplier with a system that is 99.9 percent reliable must expect and plan for a system failure. Senior management may be unaware of the need to maintain detailed back-up plans for systems and data. Only a select few in the if department may consider systems recovery as a primary function in the event of a disaster.

Disaster Categories

320 Recoveries Supported

Hardware Problems	24%
Power Outage	16%
Hurricane	16%
Flood	15%
Miscellaneous	12%
Fire / Explosion	7%
Bomb	5%
Earthquake	5%

Source: Comdisco

Almost all hospitality companies have one main database for reservations and guest history. Both are at risk if a disaster occurs. In addition, the industry's reliance on technology and communication creates several less traditional risks. The global distribution system, the importance of customer data, productivity heavily reliant on terminals and information, and the long-term effect on loyalty of a single negative experience, are additional risks particularly present in the hospitality industry.

In addition, companies are racing to build information about customer and spending patterns, investing millions of dollars in systems to institutionalize this knowledge. Loss of these systems and databases is analogous to organizational memory' loss. While rebuilding physical property may take several years, guest loyalty and behavioral history' may often require more time and money.

Disaster Recovery Plan

Clearly, the development of a technology disaster recovery' plan is an essential part of any company/s risk management program. Its development and documentation at a minimum will require the following steps:

Take an Inventory: Include items critical to the business, including the reservation system, database and the systems that support it. Telecommunications (dial-up lines, frame relay, dedicated lines and the Internet) can be included as support systems.

Assess Unavailability: Assess what will occur if critical systems are absent over specific periods of time. Ask key questions for each system. What foreseeable impact exists if accounting functionality is down, for example, or the property management system applications are non-responsive? Determine the maximum amount of downtime for these critical items before there will be a significant impact on the business.

Identify Alternatives: Identify disaster recovery alternatives for critical functions. Hospitality companies might decide that a "hot site" is a reasonable alternative with the loss of a reservation system. A hot site is a computer and data processing centre with computers in place and waiting to be used by a company experiencing a disaster. Most hot sites are permanent facilities where the company can recreate its computing environment.

Determine Alternative Requirements: Identify what is needed for an alternative to be implemented. Minimum requirements may involve telecommunications with certain bandwidths or dial-up lines. A specified level of power redundancy may be required for servers. Agreements with hardware vendors or vendors who provide disaster recovery sites may also be an option.

Identify Costs: Gain an understanding of the total cost for each alternative. Examples of common costs include arranging hardware agreements with vendors or the cost of having a disaster recovery site available for use. Installation fees, purchase of redundant telecommunications, and the purchase of upgrading telecommunications (i.e., increasing bandwidth) are other common costs. Some hospitality companies may have additional costs relating to reservation system development time as a minimum alternative requirement. **Estimate the Recovery Period:** Estimate the amount of time until the critical systems become available. Each alternative should have a specified recovery period.

Define the Limitations: Determine the limitations of each system back-up or alternative, including vendor agreements or hot sites. The plan needs to address questions of hardware replacement, especially if it is rare, discontinued, or a lag time exists between the purchase order and its delivery. The cost of an alternative or the length of time until availability may also be limitations.

Determine the Benefits: Weigh the benefits of each alternative. Use the benefits of a faster recovery in the event of a disaster as a competitive advantage. **Test the Plan Annually:** Document the test and test results as a best practice to provide a record of any problems encountered and their resolution. **IT Training in Disaster Recovery:** Provide proper training of IT personnel for implementation of the disaster recovery plan.

When a disaster or hardware failure does occur, planning rigor will make all the difference in the speed of recovery. A completed disaster recovery plan for technology systems allows companies to realize large returns on a relatively small investment-minimizing what may otherwise be an unnecessary and costly outcome of disasters.

HOTEL STRATEGIES AFTER CONSOLIDATION

The pace of consolidation within the global hotel industry has quickened in the last year. The resulting organisations are now concentrating their resources on how to develop and add further value to their existing and inherited brands. The strategies of Bass Hotels and Resorts, Starwood Lodging and Patriot American Hospitality illustrate the priority that hotel companies give to increasing brand awareness in a competitive marketplace.

Bass Hotels and Resorts

At a recent conference in New Orleans, it was confirmed that Bass Hotels and Resorts (BHR) will continue to focus on brand preference and the distribution of each chain in its relevant market. BHR is also planning a significant investment and aggressive expansion. Some US$1 billion is destined for the Inter-Continental brand, whilst increased advertising and promotion of loyalty schemes will enhance the market's awareness of the company 5 other brands, in particular Holiday Inn Express and Staybridge Suites. The company is also focusing on boosting its presence in the Middle East with several major projects under construction in Egypt, further expansion in Saudi Arabia, and a number of developments in Lebanon and Jordan.

Starwood Lodging

Following the acquisition of Sheraton and Westin, Starwood has invested US$400 million in its portfolio. During the first half of 1998, 49 management agreements were signed with a further 20 scheduled for the latter part of the year. Twenty-two hotels have been converted to the Westin or Four Points brands. For the new brand, sites under construction include five in North America, three in New York, one in Seattle and one in San Francisco. Starwood also announced that it will be combining its REIT and Starwood Hotels and Resorts to create a single C-corp with the REIT as a subsidiary. This allows the corporation to work around the change in federal law that precludes "paired share" REITs from growing through future asset acquisitions.

During the third quarter of 1998, 19 hotels were converted to the Wyndham brand, and Patriot predicts that the brand will have grown from 78 units at the beginning of the year to 185 owned or managed properties by December 1998. During the second quarter, nine former Grand Heritage hotels were repositioned as part of the Wyndham Grand Heritage brand. In the meantime, the luxury hotel division, which currently consists of 11 properties, will be branded Grand Bay Hotels and Resorts. The existing Carefree Resorts, Grand Bay Hotels and Golden Door Spa will he folded into this new operation. The roll-out of this brand will be limited to between 25 and 30 hotels in the next five years to maintain the exclusivity of the product.

Gambling

Whilst the rest of the world looks cautiously to the future and development plans are put on hold or scaled down, Las Vegas is once again breaking the mold. During the next two and a half years, 20,000 new rooms will be added. A large percentage of these are in the form of "mega-hotels" such as Hilton's "Paris' property with replicas of the Eiffel Tower and Arc de Triomphe. The scale of this new building boom is significant in itself, but the fact that it is occurring at a time of such global economic uncertainty, has raised questions about the scale of development.

There is also the added worry that the local hotel market has softened somewhat, with occupancy rates now at 86 percent compared with more than 90 percent two years ago. These levels are, of course, still extremely high, but when companies operate on the assumption of full capacity it becomes a significant drop. The turmoil in the Asian market is also taking its toll, especially with the intentional high rolling gamblers. In addition, Las Vegas 10 years ago had a monopoly in legalised gambling; today additional jurisdictions have legalised gambling. The competition is getting tougher. In an attempt to attract more families to

Las Vegas in the early years of this decade, the city introduced Disney-style entertainment, but gambling and other forms of themed entertainment do not always combine well and the results have been somewhat mixed.

... and for the rest of the world?

In spite of concerns over current and future trading conditions, many hotel companies are considering further investment and expansion across the world. Recent announcements include.

Following a 22 percent increase in profit for the six months to June 1998, U.K.-based Millennium & Copthorne Hotels has announced expansion plans. These are said to include continental Europe and gateway cities in the United States, such as Chicago, Los Angeles, Washington DC, Dallas and Atlanta.

Paris-based Accor SA is undergoing an aggressive expansion plan in Europe and South America. In Poland, the company is seeking to establish subsidiaries and joint venture partners to assist them in their development plan in central Europe. There are to be over 25 Ibis properties within the next two years. The company hopes to establish a network of over 30 Etap budget hotels during the next five years. In Brazil, Accor aims to have developed 5,500 rooms in 40 cities by the year 2002 with an initial investment of US$21 million.

Accor is also continuing its interest in expanding into Asia. Speculation continues over their interest in bidding for Century International. It has been reported in the French press that Accor is interested in expanding via the partial acquisition of Hong Kong-based Regal Hotels International.

For the first nine months of 1998, Starwood announced a 7 percent increase in revenue per available room (RevPar) for their owned hotels worldwide, with increases in Europe, Latin America and North America of 14 percent, 8 percent and 6 percent respectively.

This resulted in a 14 percent increase in EBITDA. The casino operation faired equally well with an increase in revenues of 28 percent. Starwood's development plans not only include the hotels division, but also the casino group. By the year 2000 there will be a Caesar's riverboat in Indiana, USA with 90,000 square feet of casino space and a 500-room hotel. A joint venture in Johannesburg, South Africa with Guateng will create 75,000 square feet of casino space and a 200-room hotel.

For the lodging brands of Marriott International in the United States for quarter three, RevPar grew by 5 percent compared with the previous year. Results for the international properties were moderately lower in 1998 due to the difficult trading conditions in the Asia-Pacific region. This dip was partially offset by profit growth in Europe, the Middle East and Latin America. However, the company expects to increase its portfolio by more than 150,000 rooms during the next five years, 30,000 of which are to open in 1998 within 200 hotels.

Utilising US$500 million of equity, Swissotel is eager to increase its current portfolio of 24 hotels to 60 properties by the year 2000. Currently the portfolio covers five continents with hotels concentrated in the main business centres and resort areas. For the future, Swissotel is seeking a presence in Los Angeles, San Francisco, Miami, London, Paris, Singapore, Hong Kong and Tokyo. One may be surprised to learn that hotel companies are seeking developments in Asia, but Swissotel management reportedly believes that the economic situation in that region provides a good opportunity for growth.

In Jericho Peace the Gaming Tables

The Oasis Casino opened in September 1998 and is situated in the Jordan valley, close to the ancient town of Jericho. Operated by Casinos Austria, the recently opened US$150 million Oasis has been attracting large numbers of

Israelis. According to reports, in the first weeks after opening, at least 1,000 people each day could be seen waiting to enter the casino, which had already reached capacity. Frustrated crowds even tried to enter the premises through the staff entrance to gain a chance to try their luck at one of the 45 gambling tables and 220 slot machines.

This dramatic exposure of frustrated demand has spurred Israeli politicians to revive a governmental committee, which was appointed by late Prime Minister Yitzhak Rabin, to establish two casinos in Israel on a trial basis. The Gavish Committee has previously had to deliberate over the possible pros and cons of developing a casino in the highly popular Red Sea destination of Eilat. The initial decision on opening a casino was postponed but remains eagerly awaited by local hotel operators who are expecting strong increases in demand from visiting gamblers. The Oasis Casino is expected to generate positive side effects for the local economy, supporting the 30,000 population resident in Jericho. The casino employs some 1,000 locals, and the economic spillover from the traffic created by gamblers who come from Jerusalem and even as far as Tel Aviv is having a positive effect on the local population's attitude towards the casino. Spending in Jericho has increased considerably, which in turn has had a positive impact on a number of critics who had previously rallied against the casino prior to its opening.

U.K. Travel Industry: a Global Trend

Consolidation of the U.K. travel industry has progressed at a rapid pace during the past six months. The greatest level of activity has been witnessed by the major players, as they aim to fight off competition by increasing market share and the number of distribution channels in existing markets, or obtain footholds in new markets.

Some examples of major deals in recent months include:

- Acquisition of Unijet and Hayes & Jarvis by First Choice for £134 million in June 1998;

- Purchase of Direct Holidays by Airtours in July 1998 for £80.7 million;
- Acquisition of Crystal Holidays by Thomson for £66.2 million in August 1998; and
- Announcement of the merger between Thomas Cook and U.S.-based Carlson in October 1998, which, if approved by the Monopolies and Mergers Commission, would create one of the world's largest leisure travel companies.

The high level of activity by the leading U.K. tour operators has forced other companies to take a closer look a t their distribution channels. In October 1998, First Choice, Britain's third largest tour operator, unveiled its new distribution strategy. In addition to purchasing retail travel agent Bakers Dolphin for £12 million and acquiring minority stakes in the regional chains Hays Travel and Holiday Express, it is also planning to open 533 new shops within the next two years.

Simultaneously, First Choice is buying a 25 percent stake in Holiday Hypermarkets. Holiday Hypermarkets is a pioneering new concept in retail travel, and it is estimated that the 10,000 square foot shops will generate fifteen times the number of bookings of an ordinary travel shop.

At the same time, U.K. companies have begun to diversify geographically through acquisitions in Northern Europe and North America. In October 1998, Airtours announced the acquisition of US-based tour operator Vacation Express for US$24.3 million. In Europe, operators are very keen to gain a foothold in Europe's largest outbound market, Germany. Airtours was the first U.K. tour operator to gain entry, with the purchase of a 29 percent stake in Frosch Touristik (FTi) and a further option to purchase the remainder in 2002. Thomson is also pursuing foreign expansion, having almost reached its maximum allowable market share in the United

Kingdom. Under U.K. law more than 25 percent market share would technically make it a moropoly and consequently in breach of the rules of the Monopolies and Mergers Commission.

According to Travel Industry Digest, Thomson is reportedly believed to lie interested in a potential alliance with Neckermann, Germany's second largest tour operator.

The current activity from the major U.K. tour operators is likely to continue, as they remain eager to gain a foothold in foreign markets. The Thomas Cook/Carlson deal indicates activity will most likely move away from takeovers into formal alliances and share swaps as a means of consolidation..

4

FUTURE HOTEL ORGANIZATION

MEANING AND DEFINITION

No hotel company operating today can be unaware of the swift pace of global change and its impact on every facet of the hospitality industry. With just five years left in this century, we can expect change to be the only constant. New business practices are evolving virtually as fast as our technologies, while resistance to change has become one of the primary causes of business failure. The specter of constant change raises fundamental questions as to the creation of shareholder wealth in a capital-constrained, highly competitive environment. How will hotel organizations build shareholder wealth, and what key drivers will result in success? What future products and services will be essential in a technology-driven, global environment marked by rising customer expectations? Moreover, what alternative approaches and skills must organizations develop to ensure market success?

The future success of hotel organizations will be driven in large part by the ability to foresee-and capitalize-on change. Beyond this truism, however, there is an urgent need to identify what will be required in the competitive environment of the future with its intense focus on serving customer needs. The hospitality industry-as is the case with business generally–is subject to deep currents of change set in motion as economic and social systems shaped in the industrial era evolve to a knowledge-based era driven by technology advances.

In this period of global transition, it behooves hotel organizations to examine the key factors that will not only define success, but the ability to survive in coming years. Many of these issues were spotlighted in a global study undertaken by the Economist Intelligence Unit and co-sponsored by Arthur Andersen. The Successful Corporation of the Year 2000 surveyed more than 600 senior executives around the world. Its mission was to identify the characteristics needed to lead successful businesses in the next century. These executives offer a number of compelling messages regarding the key success factors of the future.

Customers will have the strongest influence on the corporation in the year 2000. Indeed, these executives believe that the customer will be "king" in the new century. Exceptional leadership was by far the attribute most frequently cited by CEOs and senior executives; the consensus appears to be that successful companies in the year 2000 will be led by corporate visionaries.

A strategic planning focus is not only essential, but must embody a concept of planning for the future that anticipates change, rather than being based exclusively on historical models.

In structuring organizations for the future, companies must build management capabilities to deal with one of the most critical challenges diversity in the marketplace. Employing information technology to drive business success in this information-driven era is not only the path of least resistance, but vital to virtually every aspect of operations.

The study's top-line results create an excellent backdrop to address key issues confronting the hotel industry, and what factors will lead to membership–rather than rejection–in the elite club of the world's corporate success stories in the year 2000.

FOCUSING CUSTOMERS

Recognizing that the hotel industry has a somewhat split personality reflecting the inherent conflicts between its real estate and operational aspects, it is important to understand the industry's real estate origins and how they are shaping the challenges ahead. The origins of the industry's real estate persona are embodied in the classic theory of location- "if we build it, they will come."

As a result of this "building" complex, the industry has tended to have a real estate and asset orientation, rather than a customer focus. From the hotel company perspective–especially that of the brand-oriented "chain"–the varied interests of a diffused property ownership group can be quite different than the singular interest of the chain that operates and markets the properties.

Even when the ownership of geographically dispersed hotel properties is controlled by a single hotel organization, the financial structuring tends to be property-specific. Corporate financial strategies are frequently subjugated to the needs of the last property deal brought into the company's fold. Each property in a so-called "chain," is frequently the subject of a unique and distinctive ownership and financial structure. This phenomenon–quite common in the real estate sector, but unusual for business enterprises generally–makes for elusive economies of scale in the structuring and financing of property-driven expansion.

Collectively, these factors have produced low comparative returns in real estate, although criticism levelled at commercial real estate returns is somewhat less germane to the hotel industry, where management and franchise fees can produce high returns for those companies where property ownership is held by third parties. Nevertheless, average returns in the real estate industry in the United States, for example, are just over 10 percent, compared to small company stock returns at almost 20 percent and large company stocks at an average of about 15 percent.

While hotel chains have adopted traditional corporate frameworks, there are a number of predominantly real estate-driven, family-owned businesses in the hotel sector that continue to operate as relatively unstructured organizations. In meeting the future, these businesses will need plans, people and processes in order to establish viable corporate forms that can compete in tomorrow's marketplace and capitalize upon its opportunities.

In today's changed environment, the hotel organization must deal with a number of new realities. Investors in our industry are no longer satisfied with long-term capital appreciation and psychic income that heretofore were often the justification for otherwise seemingly uneconomic investments in hotel property or, indeed, hotel chains. The first reality is that there is a very specific and identifiable relationship between bottom line performance and value. Improvements in business operations raises values. It is not surprising, therefore, that the new owners attracted to this industry in recent years have new sets of demands. This transformation from an old-guard group of investors and owners to income and return-driven newcomers has meant that the once "quiet enjoyment" of operators in their management of hotels for third parties is being disturbed, interrupted and overturned.

These challenges all take place in an environment where capital has become extremely selective in markets that have little stability. A global shortage of capital will not remain a short-term problem, and future hotel organizations must have a stronger alignment to capital providers–a critical "customer" group. Hotel companies will need to compete by offering better returns and performance than in the past. Hotel chains have found their development timetables quashed in recent years, making it difficult to achieve goals of critical mass often required to improve performance.

These factors are driving consolidation in the brand "sweepstakes." Capital markets, therefore, continue to favour well-established companies, a reality that must drive entrepreneurial organizations to meet the future now by planning for an evolving corporate context in which to operate.

SUCCESS FACTORS

Within this broad context, hotel developers, owners and management companies will all need to develop new strategies, skills and processes that look forward to the competitive demands of the future. These ultimately must address issues related to vision and planning, as well as organizational skill sets and processes to attract and retain customers. To stake a claim in the future, current business practices should be examined in light of what can be expected to be the key success factors in the year 2000.

Embrace a global change orientation. As the information age produces greater worldwide integration of business activities, a global knowledge base will become invaluable. Success in local and regional hotel markets will be shaped decisively by a global business environment that defines capital movement, customer expectations and applications of new technologies. Focus on the Customer. If the customer is "king" in the 21st century, hotel organizations will be best served by focusing less on their hotel assets as measures of success, and more on their customers.

This involves a fundamental shift in viewing the real estate asset as the wealth creator–to the customer as the key to building shareholder wealth. A customer focus must imbue business decisions at all levels of developing and operating a hotel organization. Pursuing such a course will inevitably impact shareholder wealth. To accomplish this, however, customers need to participate in the product development process.

Fully realizing a customer focus in the industry poses a significant challenge. The hotel industry must confront problems due to conflicts between operational needs and real estate goals. Quite simply, an operator must remain customer-focused, but the short-term strategies to meet these needs may be inconsistent with the long-term objectives of property owners. Balancing those goals will be essential. A customer focus implies a significant shift in what drives hotel development–placing primary emphasis on the customer with the locations to follow. Nevertheless, a hotel organization with its large investment in fixed assets–the real estate–can never be as nimble as a consumer products company in adjusting products and services to match rapid shifts in the marketplace.

The Japanese taught us that the concept of "zero defects" in products and services can yield tremendous benefits. But today an even more rigorous standard dominates–quality that surprises. In practical terms, the hotel industry finds it extremely difficult to meet the standard of zero defects in service. Hotel services are based primarily on people, not computers or other equipment. Quality that surprises takes the concept of zero defects a step further. Yesterday's surprising product or service is today's status quo. Twenty years ago, a business executive did not expect a consistent and predictable level of service wherever he or she travelled in the world. Today that is a standard–not the exception–as is the expectation for sophisticated technology in hotel rooms to support business needs. With customer discrimination so acute, it is not surprising that brand loyalty is a diminishing "commodity" in the hotel industry.

Find the ingredients for visionary leadership. Today's hotel organizations need to recognize the need for visionary leadership. The ability to forecast the future–to anticipate change rather than react to it–will be one of the single greatest determinants of market dominance in the years ahead. The old "command and control" model of leadership is giving way to a focus on leadership in ideas, information, inspiration, vision and teamwork. Warren Bennis, an authority on leadership in the U.S., puts it this way–"For the most part, failing organizations tend to be over-managed and under-led. The leader sets the tone for the moral character, the vision, the corporate culture and the fiber of the institution."

While visionary leadership is essential, it must be linked to business operations and foster a risk bias, rather than a procedural bias. This will allow the organization to stretch and, in turn, change. And it must be shared by empowered professionals and staff throughout the organization, including those who meet the customer. Overcoming the resistance to change can be a daunting task, particularly in large hotel organizations in which diversions from the status quo may threaten established management lines. It suggests that a culture based on conformance may need to be replaced by an emphasis on flexibility, learning and cooperation.

Management competencies will need to be aligned in order to achieve the desired result. For many organizations, this may mean a shift from traditional hierarchies typical of companies in an industrial era to a flatter organization with a more transparent interface between leadership, organizational functions and employees. Create a defensible position through corporate strategy. For many of the industry's leaders, vision is driven by the strategic planning process, a function which has become critical for success.

Strategic planning, however, has at times been a step-child in the hotel industry, and it is often the first to be cut when organizations are downsized. It is clearly in transition. There also has been a tendency to decentralize and simplify this function–both actions of potential benefit. Strategic planning must be led by the top people in the organization–the CEO and COO. On the other hand, it should be close enough to the customer to ensure that planners can "listen" to and be influenced by customer needs.

Empower Management. Beyond the ability to envision the future, core management capabilities will make the difference–they are essential. A clear vision without the management skills to support it cannot be a recipe for success.

First and foremost, hotel management must have strategic development skills and the ability to integrate complex factors affecting success. Market volatility has become the norm, in part caused by the rapidly changing tastes of customers. Customers are increasingly approaching the hotel industry with widely different social, economic and political backgrounds, to say nothing of employees. Being able to deal with these diversities in a positive and constructive fashion that capitalizes on the differences, rather than working to find ways to mitigate them, is the clear path for successful management in the future.

The organization will also need to be imbued with a sense of entrepreneurship that reacts proactively to the market's diversity. Traditional organizations that follow well-documented rules must give way to leaders who can balance a sense of discipline with that of flexibility. Talent and resources must be marshalled and leveraged. In an industry with high fixed costs and labour intensity, the concept of leverage in the hotel business is an all-important one. Improving labour productivity through technology must be a goal for today's forward-looking hotel organization. Management must also be able to narrow the gap between the employer and the employee, forcing a flatter organization in the process. This will put management closer to the customer and speed the two-way communication process up and down the organization.

Be in the information fast lane. The traditional role of information technology (IT) as a back office support for accounting and bookkeeping has clearly moved front and centre stage. IT today influences all aspects of business from corporate strategies to organizational structure–and from the very business processes it is designed to support to performance measurement. In a world where the customer is "king," IT must also deliver in two critical areas: sales and marketing and customer service. Technology was once viewed as a way to reduce costs by replacing people. That attitude has been firmly supplanted by one that seeks IT support for the creative work that all organizations must pursue. IT must allow organizations to react more speedily to market needs and, of course, produce the fulfilment of customer demands both quickly and accurately. To do this IT must operate on a decentralized basis. IT delivers, but it has to be the right information to the right people, and it needs to be done on a timely basis.

E-PROCUREMENT IN HOSPITALITY

Models and Strategies

The hospitality industry has historically struggled under the weight of fragmented supply chains, made even more unwieldy by complex and inefficient business processes in distribution and procurement. Now that fragmentation may be put right as old economy hospitality companies turn to e-Business startups to move procurement and distribution processes online. In short, e-Procurement offers the potential for improving both ends of the equation to reduce costs, generate new revenue streams and improve audit control.

The Internet has not only fired the first shot of this revolution, it continues to be reinvented as a way for buyers to meet suppliers, and competitors to compete or partner online in efficient and cost-effective ways. As a ubiquitous global network, the Internet makes it possible to package, distribute and consume information in digital form, breaking the economic bottle-neck imposed by the production, market exchange and distribution of goods.

Digital marketplaces furnishing diverse products and services are breaking down trade barriers and offering access to hospitality companies of all sizes. Deutsche Bank currently estimates a $60 billion domestic and $100 billion international market for hospitality e-Procurement, including furniture, fixtures and equipment (FF&E), renovation and construction, service contracts, operating supplies and food and beverage (F&B). Cost savings from more efficient supply chain transactions are currently estimated to be at $3.5 billion to $4 billion in the United States alone, and $7 billion globally. Hospitality procurement of more than $20 billion domestically and $10 billion internationally is forecast to be on-line in the next 12 to 18 months

Growth in hospitality e-Procurement is clearly explosive in its potential, and our view is that hotel organizations will need to respond to this new market to remain competitive. Nevertheless, there are major obstacles to the industry seizing the advantages of e-Procurement and realizing improvements in the supply chain. This article examines marketplace models and strategies for e-Procurement as part of our series in the Hospitality and Leisure Executive Report on eBusiness opportunities.

The Internet and e-Procurement

The Internet's ability to deliver information in a common format to a wide array of computers enables businesses to access and share information from many sources-including their customers, financial institutions and suppliers. e-Procurement is a direct outgrowth of that capability. As a global network using standardized protocols and universal connectivity, the Internet opens the door for businesses to develop international marketplaces for their products and services.

Not only does the Internet facilitate the sharing of information, it simplifies the process for the end-user as well, and reduces infrastructure and transaction costs. The shared nature of the Internet distributes the infrastructure costs across large groups of potential customers, suppliers and others. That means businesses of any size can gain access for a variety of purposes. Distributors or suppliers can build revenue while also realizing reduced customer contact costs. Rather than maintaining multiple sales contact systems, suppliers need to have just one connection to the Internet.

What is the real potential for hospitality companies? e-Procurement will have a positive impact on business functions and processes for those organizations that fully take advantage of these capabilities. Buyers, for example, have a growing amount of information available to identify the suppliers with whom they want to do business. e-Procurement facilitates the aggregation of small purchases, thereby making the order process more efficient and cost effective. And it minimizes the need for intermediaries between the supplier and buyer. Traditional supply chain distributors, as a result, are being forced to provide value-added services to remain viable in the chain.

THE NEXT GENERATION

We begin by defining e-Procurement. Using digitized processes, the procurement process is engineered in concert with an all-electronic design and implementation of the infrastructure required to source, supply, manage and control services. It is one of the most important of business-to-business (B2B) functions.

e-Procurement solutions were initially launched by companies such as Ariba, Inc., which developed corporate procurement systems for global 2000 companies to give their employees access to vendors electronically. Though effective, these applications centering on "buy-side" solutions were inherently expensive and time-consuming to implement.

The new generation of e-Procurement is more revolutionary. Today, digital marketplaces create Internet portals to serve multiple buyers and sellers in the exchange of goods and services. These new ventures are levelling the playing field for both buyers and suppliers, giving smaller companies and those around the world ready access, using a Web browser, to opportunities once available primarily to larger companies in North America. Large up-front investments in hardware and software are unnecessary.

Emerging Marketplace Models

To participate in the development of e-Procurement offerings, hospitality companies will benefit by understanding the emerging digital marketplace models. Our firm's analysis indicates that there are currently two dominant models:

Industry-specific Marketplaces

Organizations with domain expertise in a particular industry-or industry "vertical" in the language of the new economy-launch these exchanges. These market-places support commerce specific to an industry as they seek to aggregate buyers and sellers to reduce transaction costs. Their competitive advantage is based on a unique understanding of industry inefficiencies. Examples can be seen in Marriott International's and Hyatt's P-Co-a joint, independent electronic purchasing network powered by GoCo-op's eCommerce engine-that leverages economies of scale to reduce prices on product and services. Or consider Instill Corporation, which links food service operators and food service product distributors/manufacturers. Instill bundles e-Procurement services to improve control and management of foodservice purchasing, offers a consolidated purchase information service for monitoring contract compliance and capturing rebates, provides market intelligence to manufacturers, and creates an online community and marketplace for small chains and independent operators to improve their operating and financial performance.

Horizontal Marketplaces

These exchanges provide a vehicle for many types of buyers and sellers to advertise, share content, bid on products, participate in auctions and manage their supply chains. Such marketplace sites serve a wide range of disparate industries and/or provide them with access to horizontal applications.

Unlike the original e-Procurement systems, which generally provided static catalogues and limited sourcing capability, these new digital marketplaces use dynamic pricing models-primarily auctions or exchanges-which are based on demand.

Horizontal marketplaces have multiple revenue streams, the most common of which come from advertising on sites. Many of these marketplaces also generate revenues in the form of commissions charged to sellers participating in auctions. Storefront sales to sellers can be an additional source of revenue for such marketplaces. Tradeout.com, one such example of a horizontal marketplace, categorizes its services to multiple industries by product type. Its services include the hosting of seller-driven auctions for excess inventory resale. In such auctions, sellers list their products and receive price bids from multiple buyers for individual products, thereby enabling the seller to potentially receive the highest price for their products, including any excess inventory that ordinarily would have to be written off. Vertical marketplaces have similar revenue sources, although they are able to command higher advertising fees due to the detailed information they can collect on concentrated groups of members and subscribers. Additionally, some of them also generate revenues by charging subscription fees to access their focused content and product data.

In contrast to vertical marketplaces, horizontal marketplaces face challenges specific to their broad mission. Based on the need to appeal to diverse industries, these marketplaces must satisfy the product, service and content needs of their varied buyers and members, and may be fighting an uphill battle in doing so. Some companies have been successful using this model, but they have had to invest in expensive domain experts to develop the compelling offerings typically available in a vertical marketplace. The diversity of the industries served by horizontal marketplaces, however, can be useful in reducing risk in the event of limited penetration in a particular vertical.

A hybrid marketplace model is beginning to emerge with the advantage of leveraging the strengths of both models. In this model several contiguous verticals are represented in a marketplace. These contiguous verticals can be grouped according to the similar products and services used by all, yet still maintain the content and other offerings unique to each. A hybrid market-place, for example, might provide an exchange for food service, hospitality and grocery industry members, which could be grouped together to access food and beverage suppliers. In contrast, hospitality industry member sites might feature only FF&E items, such as beds. Buyers can benefit from hybrid models of digital marketplaces because they can potentially access more sellers and therefore have more bargaining power.

Similarly, marketplaces are expanding internationally, according to Forrester Research, despite barriers in some countries to Internet adoption, including public policies impeding imports and exports. Global expansion boosts supplier access to new markets and exposes new buyers to eBusiness. Although North America will own half of all online sales in 2004, reports Forrester, eBusiness in Western Europe will grow to $1.5 trillion, followed by Latin America, which is projected to reach $82 billion in 2004. Developing countries such as Zimbabwe are not projected to have eBusiness begin to take off until after 2010

The Implications of e-Procurement

e-Procurement clearly offers significant opportunities for hospitality industry players to improve their supply chains, and those companies that ignore the potential may suffer in the long run. During these early stages of the e-Procurement revolution, relationships among buyers, sellers and competitors will be redefined.

Additionally, global eBusiness will be fuelled by the ability to track the movement of trade goods at any point along the supply chain. Ships transporting goods from Latin America to North America, for example, might be quickly redirected to Europe in the event that bids were greater in other locations. Such flexibility in real-time pricing would greatly minimize reliance on fixed prices.

We can summarize the implications for various segments of the hospitality industry in the following points:

Brand Names

- Established brands can leverage their relationships, experience, knowledge and purchasing power to reengineer corporate purchasing efforts for improved efficiency.
- These players can develop (or partner with vendors and/or with competitors) private, secure, customized sites for employees to purchase products and services from approved vendors. Real-time inventory management and accounting then becomes possible.
- The major brands can also take control of the procurement process by minimizing "maverick" purchases and monitoring adherence to approved vendor lists, ensuring their employees adhere to quality standards.

Management Companies and Independents

- These companies will gain access to rebates traditionally only available to larger companies based on aggregated demand.
- The buying power of hotels outside North America, which have had little clout historically, should be increased.
- Management will be able to leverage public access applications that provide access to extensive vendor

networks and their products in horizontal or vertical marketplaces.

- Moving processes online should result in labour cost savings.

Outlook for the Future

To fully leverage the benefits of end-to-end e-Procurement, hospitality companies need to position procurement more strategically and demand value-added services from providers to manage the entire supply chain from requisition to payment. Customer care services-a critical component of these solutions-must be situated throughout the supply chain to enable hospitality companies to realize the full benefits. Consolidated reporting will also be important.

Market forces are promoting marketplaces that encompass several contiguous verticals, rather than a single vertical focus of products or services. In hybrid market-place exchanges, managers of individual verticals will continue to need a great deal of domain expertise. However, they will also be able to cross-pollinate and leverage the capabilities of other market-places to benefit each one of their industries individually. This will promote e-Procurement offerings that are moving toward one-stop shopping, while providing vertical-specific services.

In the medium-term we anticipate that eBusiness ecosystems will emerge as the next wave of e-Procurement solutions. These interconnected worlds will allow organizations (employees, suppliers and customers) to transact via a single point for commerce and information, creating a global web of digital markets and corporate exchanges. This new wave of development will provide hospitality companies with clear benefits:

- Competitive and dynamic pricing.
- Ability to customize marketplaces. This will result in minimized searching costs through vendor-specific

interfaces to facilitate adherence to quality standards and vendor comparison.

- Consolidated reporting and accounting to monitor supply chain performance and improve budgeting.
- Single point of contact for customer care.
- Access to international distribution networks.
- Process improvements in handling purchase orders.
- Customized online order-flow-tracking capability that is based on a company's internal workflow routing process.
- Streamlined buyer and supplier commerce processes.
- Shared network of commerce services.
- New methods of dynamic sourcing and trade.
- Aggregated purchasing and expanded sales channels.
- Extended customer reach and enhanced customer service.
- Meaningful tools to facilitate marketplace interaction.

To fully leverage the benefits of end-to-end e-Procurement, hospitality companies need to position procurement, hospitality companies need to position procurement more strategically and demand value-added services from providers to manage the entire supply chain from requisition to payment.

SUMMATIVE ANALYSIS

Despite the benefits promoted by e-Procurement marketplaces, the industry may be slow to adopt full-fledged solutions. The reasons for that are varied, but they include the large investments in legacy systems; bandwidth scalability and reliability issues associated with the Internet; and resistance to changing procedures and learning new systems. Deutsche Bank warns that e-Procurement cost savings may not be fully realized by the industry for another reason. An increase in e-Procurement marketplaces may decrease the likelihood of an industry platform standard for electronic commerce, thereby reducing the ability of suppliers and buyers to interact on multiple platforms and potentially minimizing cost savings.

Privacy and security issues will also be major issues, particularly in the case of market-places developed by industry leaders. Those hospitality companies interested in such solutions will most likely be wary about exposing their key business functions to competitors. Solution providers will also have to protect against vulnerability to hackers and competitors.

To fully realize the benefits of eBusiness in general and e-Procurement in particular, hospitality organizations will need to:

- Determine how to integrate their overall business strategy with the eBusiness ecosystem.
- Identify and weigh the impact on the organization (traditional processes will be affected significantly).
  - How will our traditional "requisition-to-pay" process be affected?
- Ask the following questions to determine how to best integrate eBusiness systems/solutions with existing legacy/back-office/front-office systems.

* What systems are still necessary?
* What skill sets do we need to acquire?

- Ask for answers in key areas as part of evaluating whether to leverage the Application Service Provider model:

* Does your company have a shortage in internal IT skills?
* Are there any upfront costs to buyer (subscription fee model)?

* Will the ASP partner assume responsibility for managing the application?
* Will the ASP services free resources to be focused on other areas deemed more critical to your core business?

e-Procurement offers a bright promise of reduced transaction costs and greater efficiencies for hospitality companies. While there are obstacles, it's clear that the success stories of the new economy will increasingly involve companies that use e-Procurement to their own competitive advantage on the global stage.

5

THE HOTEL MARKETS

TRENDS OF THE HOTEL MARKET

Tokyo

	1993	1994	1995	1996	1997
No. of Hotels	17	19	20	21	21
No. of Rooms	12,079	12,769	13,108	13,557	13,557
A Year Rooms Supply	4,408,835	4,500,059	4,702,043	4,929,699	4,948,305
A Year Rooms Demand	2,968,799	3,101,397	3,165,160	3,632,409	3,751,583
Occupancy	67.3%	68.9%	67.3%	73.7%	75.8%
Average Daily Rate (yen)	24,610	22,590	21,917	21,565	22,198

Japan's hotel markets are diverse as they span the country's four main islands that extend in a crescent shaped archipelago in the north Pacific. The following summarizes characteristics of eight hotel markets, the largest in Japan, beginning with the nation's capital, Tokyo.

One of the world's largest cities, Tokyo stands as the centre for Japan's economic and administrative functions, as well as affairs related to political, government, finance, international trade and corporate headquarters. As a result, the Tokyo hotel market is most resilient for every segment, including out-bound, in-bound and regional travellers and consumers. Even with a distressed economy, room demand has surpassed rooms supply. Tokyo also enjoys a double-digit share of the foreigner guests. In the upper-tier properties in Tokyo, room night demand generated by foreign guests exceeds 50 percent of total demand.

A bullish economy in the late 1980s motivated investments in major additions to the high-end hotel market, which came online in the 1990s. Four Seasons Tokyo (1992, 283 rooms); The Westin Tokyo (1994, 444 rooms); Hotel Inter-Continental Tokyo Bay, (1995, 339 rooms); Hotel Nikko Tokyo (1996, 453 rooms); and Park Hyatt (1994, 178 rooms); and Le Meridien Grand Pacific Tokyo (1998, 884 rooms) are good examples of these developments. These new luxury entries increased Tokyo's rooms inventory in the first-tier market 15.9 percent between 1993 and 1998, while demand increased by 26.9 percent during the same period.

Tokyo hotels, however, have not avoided all of the downside of the current economy where losses are seen in the high-volume banquet and restaurant business. The rooms revenue of the typical full-service first class hotels of 200 rooms or more is typically less than 30 percent of the Gross Operating Revenue (GOR), while at the same time the banquet and F&B can easily sell 60 percent or more of GOR. The shrinkage of the gross market size in Tokyo hotels in aggregate revenue is believed to exceed 30 percent during the last five years of recession. Most of that market shrinkage is in the banquet and restaurant business, reflecting weakened corporate business sponsors.

Osaka

The Osaka prefecture recently suffered from the largest fiscal deficit at the level of the prefecture government. Many of the area developments have been suspended given the cumulative loss incurred from uncompleted development projects. Kansai New International Airport with only a single runway is so far not generating an expected volume of the inbound arrivals. The bay area developments, including Universal

Studio Japan, seem to be among the very few projects to help the Osaka hotel market to correct the current oversupply. In particular, the new luxury entries (e.g., The Imperial, The Westin, Hankyu International and Ritz Carlton) are said to be particularly affected by the slow economy.

1st Tier Hotel Market Trend

Osaka

	1993	1994	1995	1996	1997
No. of Hotels	9	10	10	11	12
No. of Rooms	4,785	5,411	5,411	5,798	6,090
A Year Rooms Supply	1,746,525	1,888,015	1,975,015	2,093,430	2,181,386
A Year Rooms Demand	1,094,612	1,287,157	1,524,876	1,586,068	1,634,953
Occupancy	62.7%	68.2%	77.2%	75.8%	75.0%
Averge Daily Rate (yen)	18,037	16,466	15,703	15,124	15,114

Source: Arthur Andersen Hospitality & Leisure Services, Tokyo

Yokohama

The city is the second largest in Japan in population, and yet is still only one-third the size of Tokyo. The romantic port town atmosphere supported by new area development-including the spectacular bay bridge, international convention centre and the Landmark Tower building-has stimulated new hotel demand. However, as long as the hotels must target the leisure market, which naturally tends to be concentrated to the weekends and holidays, without increasing support in the business segment, Yokohama hoteliers will continue to suffer from reduced demand. The competition among the hotel neighbours lined up along the new bay area called MM21 will remain intense. In addition, new competition also arrived last year with the opening of the Tokyo Bay Sheraton Yokohama in June 1998.

Kyoto

Just 20 minutes away from Osaka by Shinkansen or bullet train, Kyoto is Japan's best known tourist destination for both overseas and domestic tourists. As such, its hotel market tends to be self-sustaining.

While the hotel market has not posted a downward trend, it remains weak, however.

1st Tier Hotel Market Trend
Kyoto

	1993	1994	1995	1996	1997
No. of Hotels	10	12	12	12	13
No. of Rooms	3,291	3,836	3,836	3,829	4,008
A Year Rooms Supply	1,201,215	1,198,678	1,400,140	1,401,414	1,417,398
A Year Rooms Demand	796,936	937,177	925,412	976,381	1,008433
Occupancy	66.3%	78.2%	66.1%	69.7%	71.1%
Average Daily Rate (yen)	16,072	15,909	16,223	16,019	15,817

Source: Arthur Andersen Hospitality & Leisure Services, Tokyo

Sapporo

This is the capital city of Hokkaido, the island prefecture situated at Japan's northern territory, which is suffering from a weak regional economy. Hokkaido Takushoku Bank, one of the large commercial

banks headquartered in Sapporo, was the first bank bankruptcy in Japan under "Japanese Financial Big Bang". The city's hotel operators depend on business travel driven from local branch offices of the corporations based in Tokyo and Osaka. But the primary room demand comes from tourism, which reflects strong seasonal fluctuations. As a result, Sapporo hotels have limited average room turnover due to the seasonal fluctuation and low ADR depressed by the dominant bargaining power of travel agents.

Kobe

Like Osaka, Kobe has a large international port with an exotic and romantic ambience, and has long attracted leisure visitors from nearby Yokohama. Kobe, however, continues to recover from the 1995 earthquake, the largest in Japan since 1923. And this recovery has been slower due to the national economy. Kobe tourism, however, has recovered in terms of tourist arrivals.

Nagoya

This city seems to have a better socio-economic outlook compared to the other major "branch-economy" cities in Japan. The city has avoided becoming an economic subsidiary to Tokyo or Osaka, even though main factory lines of Toyota contribute to stabilizing the regional economy. Nagoya will be the host city for the World Exposition expected to be held in year 2005. Also, a new Nagoya international airport is in preliminary survey. Unlike other major cities in Japan, Nagoya avoided the hotel industry recession until recently when rapid increases in the room supply resulted in very tight competition. The competition is expected to become more heated when JR Tokai opens The Nagoya Marriott Associa Hotel in May 2000 with 780 rooms and 17 banquet halls, nine restaurants and wedding facilities.

Fukuoka

Fukuoka City serves as the capital of Fukuoka prefecture, as well as the gateway city to Kyushyu Island, located to the southwest of the main island (Honshu). Like Sapporo,

Fukuoka City hosts many branch offices of Tokyo-based corporations. It also maintains close communications and traffic with nearby Asian countries such as Korea, China, Taiwan and Hong Kong, which have become feeder markets of tourists inbound to Kyushu. Reduced travel among Asia nations as a result of recession has had an impact on Fukuoka's hotel market. But a strong mix of tourism resources-the local culture, sea food, tourist points of the sea and mountains, abundant hot springs and large theme parks-also attract leisure tourists from the neighbouring Japanese prefectures of Ohita, Kumamoto, Miyazaki and Kagoshima. Business and conference are also important travel segments. Fukuoka accommodates the most number of medical related conventions in Japan through a year.

6

SUCCESSFUL MANAGEMENT

THE TAJ

Taj Hotels Resorts and Palaces is the largest Indian luxury hotel chain. A wholly owned subsidiary of the Tata Group, Taj Hotels Resort and Palaces comprises 57 hotels in 39 locations across India with an additional 18 international hotels in the Maldives, Mauritius, Malaysia, Seychelles, United Kingdom, United States of America, Bhutan, Sri Lanka, Africa, the Middle East and Australia.

Their first and most well known property is the Taj Mahal Palace & Tower in Colaba, Mumbai. The Taj Mahal Palace & Tower, Mumbai was opened on December 16, 1903, by the founder of the Tata Group, Jamshetji Nusserwanji Tata. Taj President-a business hotel and Taj Land's End-an ultimate luxury boarding are also located in Mumbai.

It operates TajAir, a luxury private jet operation with state-of-the-art Falcon 2000 aircraft designed by Dassault Aviation, France; and Taj Yachts, two 3-bedroom luxury yachts which can be used by guests in Mumbai and Kochi.

FALAKNUMA PALACE

Falaknuma Palace is situated on a hill 650 meters in height, in the Old City of Hyderabad, India. It was built by Nawab Vikar-ul-Umra. It was purchased by the then Nizam VI during 1897 for use as a royal guest house. The palace provides a good view of Hyderabad. The palace is spread out in a scorpion shape with two pincers spread out as wings on the north. The middle part occupies the main building. The Harem quarters and the kitchen stretch towards the south.

The palace was designed by an Italian architect. The palace boasts of lavishly decorated interiors made of the Italian marble, and follows a western architectural style. It took almost nine years to complete. This famous palace houses a large collection of rare treasures, paintings, statues, furniture, manuscripts and books collected by the Nizam. The jade collection displayed here is considered to be unique in the world. Some old models of artillery are also exhibited in the front. The Palace is being converted into a heritage hotel by the Taj Hotels group.

FUTURE TRENDS

No hotel company operating today can be unaware of the swift pace of global change and its impact on every facet of the hospitality industry. With just five years left in this century, we can expect change to be the only constant. New business practices are evolving virtually as fast as our technologies, while resistance to change has become one of the primary causes of business failure.

The specter of constant change raises fundamental questions as to the creation of shareholder wealth in a capital-constrained, highly competitive environment. How will hotel organizations build shareholder wealth, and what key drivers will result in success? What future products and services will be essential in a technology-driven, global environment marked by rising customer expectations? Moreover, what alternative approaches and skills must organizations develop to ensure market success?

The future success of hotel organizations will be driven in large part by the ability to foresee--and capitalize--on change. Beyond this truism, however, there is an urgent need to identify what will be required in the competitive environment of the future with its intense focus on serving customer needs. The hospitality industry–as is the case with business generally--is subject to deep currents of change set in motion as economic and social systems shaped in the industrial era evolve to a knowledge-based era driven by technology advances.

In this period of global transition, it behooves hotel organizations to examine the key factors that will not only define success, but the ability to survive in coming years. Many of these issues were spotlighted in a global study undertaken by the Economist Intelligence Unit and co-sponsored by Arthur Andersen. The Successful Corporation of the Year 2000 surveyed more than 600 senior executives around the world. Its mission was to identify the characteristics needed to lead successful businesses in the next century. These executives offer a number of compelling messages regarding the key success factors of the future.

Customers will have the strongest influence on the corporation in the year 2000. Indeed, these executives believe that the customer will be "king" in the new century. Exceptional leadership was by far the attribute most frequently cited by CEOs and senior executives; the consensus appears to be that successful companies in the year 2000 will be led by corporate visionaries.

A strategic planning focus is not only essential, but must embody a concept of planning for the future that anticipates change, rather than being based exclusively on historical models. In structuring organizations for the future, companies must build management capabilities to deal with one of the most critical challenges–diversity in the marketplace. Employing information technology to drive business success in this information-driven era is not only the path of least resistance, but vital to virtually every aspect of operations.

The study's top-line results create an excellent backdrop to address key issues confronting the hotel industry, and what factors will lead to membership–rather than rejection–in the elite club of the world's corporate success stories in the year 2000.

CUSTOMER FOCUS

Recognizing that the hotel industry has a somewhat split personality reflecting the inherent conflicts between its real estate and operational aspects, it is important to understand the industry's real estate origins and how they are shaping the challenges ahead. The origins of the industry's real estate persona are embodied in the classic theory of location-"if we build it, they will come." As a result of this "building" complex, the industry has tended to have a real estate and asset orientation, rather than a customer focus. From the hotel company perspective–especially that of the brand-oriented "chain"–the varied interests of a diffused property ownership group can be quite different than the singular interest of the chain that operates and markets the properties.

Even when the ownership of geographically dispersed hotel properties is controlled by a single hotel organization, the financial structuring tends to be property-specific. Corporate financial strategies are frequently subjugated to the needs of the last property deal brought into the company's fold. Each property in a so-called "chain," is frequently the subject of a unique and distinctive ownership and financial structure. This phenomenon–quite common in the real estate sector, but unusual for business enterprises generally–makes for elusive economies of scale in the structuring and financing of property-driven expansion.

Collectively, these factors have produced low comparative returns in real estate, although criticism levelled at commercial real estate returns is somewhat less germane to the hotel industry, where management and franchise fees can produce high returns for those companies where property ownership is held by third parties. Nevertheless, average returns in the real estate industry in the United States, for example, are just over 10 percent, compared to small company stock returns at almost 20 percent and large company stocks at an average of about 15 percent.

While hotel chains have adopted traditional corporate frameworks, there are a number of predominantly real estate-driven, family-owned businesses in the hotel sector that continue to operate as relatively unstructured organizations. In meeting the future, these businesses will need plans, people and processes in order to establish viable corporate forms that can compete in tomorrow's marketplace and capitalize upon its opportunities.

In today's changed environment, the hotel organization must deal with a number of new realities. Investors in our industry are no longer satisfied with long-term capital appreciation and psychic income that heretofore were often the justification for otherwise seemingly uneconomic investments in hotel property or, indeed, hotel chains. The first reality is that there is a very specific and identifiable relationship between bottom line performance and value. Improvements in business operations raises values. It is not surprising, therefore, that the new owners attracted to this industry in recent years have new sets of demands. This transformation from an old-guard group of investors and owners to income and return-driven newcomers has meant that the once "quiet enjoyment" of operators in their management of hotels for third parties is being disturbed, interrupted and overturned.

These challenges all take place in an environment where capital has become extremely selective in markets that have little stability. A global shortage of capital will not remain a short-term problem, and future hotel organizations must have a stronger alignment to capital providers–a critical "customer" group. Hotel companies will need to compete by offering better returns and performance than in the past.

Hotel chains have found their development timetables quashed in recent years, making it difficult to achieve goals of critical mass often required to improve performance. These factors are driving consolidation in the brand "sweepstakes." Capital markets, therefore, continue to favour well-established companies, a reality that must drive entrepreneurial organizations to meet the future now by planning for an evolving corporate context in which to operate.

SUCCESS FACTORS

Within this broad context, hotel developers, owners and management companies will all need to develop new strategies, skills and processes that look forward to the competitive demands of the future. These ultimately must address issues related to vision and planning, as well as organizational skill sets and processes to attract and retain customers. To stake a claim in the future, current business practices should be examined in light of what can be expected to be the key success factors in the year 2000.

Embrace a global change orientation. As the information age produces greater worldwide integration of business activities, a global knowledge base will become invaluable. Success in local and regional hotel markets will be shaped decisively by a global business environment that defines capital movement, customer expectations and applications of new technologies.

Focus on the Customer

If the customer is "king" in the 21st century, hotel organizations will be best served by focusing less on their hotel assets as measures of success, and more on their customers.

This involves a fundamental shift in viewing the real estate asset as the wealth creator--to the customer as the key to building shareholder wealth. A customer focus must imbue business decisions at all levels of developing and operating a hotel organization. Pursuing such a course will inevitably impact shareholder wealth. To accomplish this, however, customers need to participate in the product development process.

Fully realizing a customer focus in the industry poses a significant challenge. The hotel industry must confront problems due to conflicts between operational needs and real estate goals. Quite simply, an operator must remain customer-focused, but the short-term strategies to meet these needs may be inconsistent with the long-term objectives of property owners. Balancing those goals will be essential. A customer focus implies a significant shift in what drives hotel development--placing primary emphasis on the customer with the locations to follow. Nevertheless, a hotel organization with its large investment in fixed assets--the real estate--can never be as nimble as a consumer products company in adjusting products and services to match rapid shifts in the marketplace.

The Japanese taught us that the concept of "zero defects" in products and services can yield tremendous benefits. But today an even more rigorous standard dominates--quality that surprises. In practical terms, the hotel industry finds it extremely difficult to meet the standard of zero defects in service. Hotel services are based primarily on people, not computers or other equipment.

Quality that surprises takes the concept of zero defects a step further. Yesterday's surprising product or service is today's status quo. Twenty years ago, a business executive did not expect a consistent and predictable level of service wherever he or she travelled in the world. Today that is a standard--not the exception--as is the expectation for sophisticated technology in hotel rooms to support business needs. With customer discrimination so acute, it is not surprising that brand loyalty is a diminishing "commodity" in the hotel industry.

Ingredients for Visionary Leadership

Today's hotel organizations need to recognize the need for visionary leadership. The ability to forecast the future--to anticipate change rather than react to it--will be one of the single greatest determinants of market dominance in the years ahead. The old "command and control" model of leadership is giving way to a focus on leadership in ideas, information, inspiration, vision and teamwork. Warren Bennis, an authority on leadership in the U.S., puts it this way--"For the most part, failing organizations tend to be over-managed and under-led. The leader sets the tone for the moral character, the vision, the corporate culture and the fiber of the institution."

While visionary leadership is essential, it must be linked to business operations and foster a risk bias, rather than a procedural bias. This will allow the organization to stretch and, in turn, change. And it must be shared by empowered professionals and staff throughout the organization, including those who meet the customer. Overcoming the resistance to change can be a daunting task, particularly in large hotel organizations in which diversions from the status quo may threaten established management lines. It suggests that a culture based on conformance may need to be replaced by an emphasis on flexibility, learning and cooperation. Management competencies will need to be aligned in order to achieve the desired result. For many organizations, this may mean a shift from traditional hierarchies typical of companies in an industrial era to a flatter organization with a more transparent interface between leadership, organizational functions and employees.

Create a defensible position through corporate strategy. For many of the industry's leaders, vision is driven by the strategic planning process, a function which has become critical for success. Strategic planning, however, has at times been a step-child in the hotel industry, and it is often the first to be cut when organizations are downsized. It is clearly in transition. There also has been a tendency to decentralize and simplify this function--both actions of potential benefit. Strategic planning must be led by the top people in the organization--the CEO and COO. On the other hand, it should be close enough to the customer to ensure that planners can "listen" to and be influenced by customer needs.

Management Empowerment

Beyond the ability to envision the future, core management capabilities will make the difference--they are essential. A clear vision without the management skills to support it cannot be a recipe for success. First and foremost, hotel management must have strategic development skills and the ability to integrate complex factors affecting success. Market volatility has become the norm, in part caused by the rapidly changing tastes of customers. Customers are increasingly approaching the hotel industry with widely different social, economic and political backgrounds, to say nothing of employees. Being able to deal with these diversities in a positive and constructive fashion that capitalizes on the differences, rather than working to find ways to mitigate them, is the clear path for successful management in the future.

The organization will also need to be imbued with a sense of entrepreneurship that reacts proactively to the market's diversity. Traditional organizations that follow well-documented rules must give way to leaders who can balance a sense of discipline with that of flexibility. Talent and resources must be marshalled and leveraged. In an industry with high fixed costs and labour intensity, the concept of leverage in the hotel business is an all-important one. Improving labour productivity through technology must be a goal for today's forward-looking hotel organization. Management must also be able to narrow the gap between the employer and the employee, forcing a flatter organization in the process. This will put management closer to the customer and speed the two-way communication process up and down the organization.

Be in the Fast Lane Information

The traditional role of information technology (IT) as a back office support for accounting and bookkeeping has clearly moved front and centre stage. IT today influences all aspects of business from corporate strategies to organizational structure--and from the very business processes it is designed to support to performance measurement. In a world where the customer is "king," IT must also deliver in two critical areas: sales and marketing and customer service.

Technology was once viewed as a way to reduce costs by replacing people. That attitude has been firmly supplanted by one that seeks IT support for the creative work that all organizations must pursue. IT must allow organizations to react more speedily to market needs and, of course, produce the fulfilment of customer demands both quickly and accurately. To do this IT must operate on a decentralized basis. IT delivers, but it has to be the right information to the right people, and it needs to be done on a timely basis.

IMPROVING THE PROJECT

Improving Management of NGO and Privately Owned Nature Reserves and High Biodiversity Islands in Seychelles Project funded by the Global Environment Facility through the World Bank

The Seychelles is known world wide as a storehouse of rare biodiversity. Historically, most of the islands and ecosystems have been severely impacted by human activities. Nevertheless, a few examples of whole island ecosystems have been protected and restored. These islands are Cousin, Cousine, Aride, Fregate and Aldabra, all managed, surprisingly, by civil society organisations. Nevertheless, there are significant barriers to sustainability of conservation efforts by these organisations.

The focus of the project is two islands, Cousin and Cousine, which are host to numerous rare and endemic species, and immense biodiversity. These include shared resources such as 10 species of breeding seabirds, 5 species of endemic land birds, rare floral species, 8 species of reptiles and hundreds species of invertebrates, the most important population of hawksbill turtles in the Western Indian Ocean and the highest biomass of reef fish in the granitic islands of Seychelles. The project is to ensure the islands' function as a reserve for the preservation of globally important biodiversity through understanding processes and changes in sites, species and habitats in the islands for better management and decision-making on activities to preserve this globally important biodiversity.

Cousin and Cousine are adjacent to Praslin-the second most populous island of the Seychelles. Cousin was purchased in the 1960's through a world wide appeal at a time when unique biodiversity in Seychelles was in jeopardy. An international NGO held the title to the island because land tenureship was the only method of securing the island for perpetuity and thereby restoring the ecosystems. This NGOs also assisted the previous owners of Cousine in the early years to conserve its biodiversity. This proved to be a very wise move because the islands are remarkable in that unlike other granitic islands of Seychelles, endemic and globally important fauna and flora have been saved.

They have been protected by NGO/private resources and management, and at least for Cousin, through national legislation and policy. The ownership and management regimes by civil society organisations and the relative remoteness, which are the main reasons why biodiversity has been saved, are now proving to be constraints for not only continuing with established activities but also for initiating new programs; the civil society organisations cannot source adequate resources from the local private sector, governmental or international sources. In addition, anthropogenic impacts and lack of knowledge of ecosystem-level changes, all mean that science and conservation action on each of them cannot move beyond present capacity and limits.

The project assumption is that conservation of island biodiversity can be sustained and at the same time greatly improved through an inter-island integrated and collaborative approach geared to clear management outcomes and also to the development of public education and community buy-in. The project recognises the importance of developing financial sustainability to maintain these conservation programs. The project intends to build long-term capacity for sustainable conservation and use of island biodiversity through program and capacity building, infrastructure acquisition and installation, co-management, and education and advocacy.

The two islands are small, close to each other, and share similar and sensitive ecosystems, associated conservation activities and problems. They are both focused on biodiversity conservation, chiefly concerning globally threatened endemic land birds and internationally important colonies of breeding seabirds. Each island also hosts similar important reptile, botanical and invertebrate species. Both islands have a distinguished conservation history and offer a slightly different model and philosophy for biodiversity conservation. Cousin Island is owned by an international NGO but managed by an independent, locally registered, not-for-profit Association. Cousine Island is owned and managed by a private limited company registered in Seychelles. Management of the islands are supposed to be undertaken with in-country resources.

VISION OF THE PROJECT

The project will remove barriers that currently prevent civil society organisations from augmenting and enhancing their capacity to conserve and restore species, sites and habitats.

The project will aims to create partnerships between neighbouring islands which have shared globally important biodiversity and similar environmental issues. This will be done through a substantial number of new and improved linked programs, the creation of a common resource and management center, institutional strengthening and capacity building, and public education and advocacy.

The ultimate aim of this model partnership is to catalyze further collaboration and public buy-in, to remove other barriers and to mitigate negative ecosystem changes. The process set in motion by the project will improve the management of high biodiversity islands as well as increase the number of managed conservation sites in Seychelles. This project will thus have global biodiversity benefits, lead to greater sustainability of biodiversity and permit the sharing of these benefits to be directed principally at local levels. The vision mirrors the three principal objectives of the 1992 Convention of Biological Diversity.

OVERALL GOAL

The Goal of the project is to improve management of biodiversity-rich islands by installing a shared multi-pronged programme framework and infrastructure for enhanced and sustainable conservation, financing and use of biodiversity. The project vision and overall goal will be delivered through two principal components namely Small Island Ecosystem Management, and Public Education and Advocacy.:.

Component 1: Small Island Ecosystem Management

A. Improved management of terrestrial and marine habitats and important species.

B. Establish collaborative management and resource center on Praslin

C. Institutional strengthening

D. Capacity building and training

Component 2: Public Education and Advocacy

A. Develop biodiversity awareness and advocacy programs

B. Establish community outreach, partnerships and stakeholder participation programs

PARTNERS OF THE PROJECT

Nature Seychelles, formerly known as BirdLife Seychelles, is a local not-for-profit association registered in Seychelles.

It is currently the largest independent environment organisation in Seychelles. The association is involved in a suite of activities including species and habit conservation, monitoring, research, island restoration, eco-tourism, education and awareness and advocacy.

Nature Seychelles manages Cousin Island Special Reserve and has a presence on several other islands. It has a multi-stakeholder and result-oriented approach through its programs such as the Seychelles Magpie-robin Recovery Team (SMART) and the Seychelles Seabird Group (SSG) as well with other organisations such as the WildLife Clubs of Seychelles, Ministry of Environment and Ministry of Education. Its donors and partners include the World Bank/ GEF and the Royal Society for Protection of Birds. It is a member of the BirdLife International network, WIOMSA, the African Bird Club and IUCN, works in close collaboration with WWF, the Mauritian WildLife Foundation and many others.

Cousine Island LTD (Owner and Manger of Cousine Island): is a private limited company registered in the Seychelles. The company has built a very small and ecologically friendly luxury hotel. The island is not legally protected and the owner is not obliged to conserve its biodiversity. The company has voluntarily put in a system for biodiversity conservation using its own resources. It delegates management responsibility for the island to a Conservation Warden. The Warden works in close collaboration with the hotel manager. The purpose of setting up the small hotel is to bring in sufficient revenues to maintain the conservation and research programs on the island and to maintain it as a high biodiversity area. The company supports other conservation programs in Seychelles, for example the Magpie Robin Recovery Program and the Seychelles Rare Birds Committee.

THE LANDMARKS

Hotel Association of India, established on 24th October 1996, within a short span of less than a decade of its inception, has successfully provided an integrated hospitality platform produced ground breaking results and recorded several notable 'firsts' for the hospitality industry described in the ensuing pages:-

Export House Status

Among the path breaking industry 'first' initiatives of Hotel Association of India is the unique recognition secured for tourism and hospitality sectors in India as 'export industries'. This was an unparelled achievement of the Association which undertook the entire groundwork and created consensus in support of according export status for hospitality industries.

HAI organized series of inter-active meetings with the concerned Ministries of the Government of India, culminating in a high level Conclave presided over by Shri Ramakrishna Hegde, then Hon'ble Minister of Commerce, Government of India, on 16th July 1998 at the Oberoi Hotel, New Delhi which cleared the decks for the action plan blue-printed by HAI receiving the official seal of approval of the Government of India manifested in the a Gazette Notification of November 26th, 1998 declaring Hotels and Tourism Units eligible for the benefits of Service Export House/International Service

Export House/International Star Service Export House/International Super Star Service Export House categories on the basis of their quantum of foreign exchange earnings.

This extraordinary recognition placed hotels and tourism units on par with industries engaged in export of products for imports of projects and products against their foreign exchange entitlements and facilitated hotels in acquiring competitive edge vis-à-vis hotels overseas in providing world class facilities.

Tourism Export Promotion Council

Another notable first for hospitality and tourism industries, synchronizing with the grant of Export House Status, was notched by the Hotel Association of India by formulating the Constitution of the Tourism Export Promotion Council (TEPC) on 20th November 1998. The approval of the Company Law Board was also secured for the new body under Section 25 of the Companies Act 1956. TEPC represented an unique experiment in bringing together for the first time all constituents of the tourism sector-hotels, travel agents, tour operators, transporters, airlines, tourism finance companies-under a single umbrella on a common platform.

SAARC Hotel Association

HAI reached beyond the national boundaries to provide regional co-operation aiming hotels in South Asia and became the prime mover in the formation of the SAARC Hotel Association. This was achieved by developing close synergy between the hospitality industry organizations of Bangladesh, Bhutan, India, Maldives, Nepal, Pakistan and Sri Lanka. The SAARC Hotel Association was formally launched at Mumbai on 7th April 1999 with Nepal being assigned the responsibility of hosting the SAARC body for its initial two years and later by rotation by other member countries.

International Code of Conduct

For the first time in the history of travel trade in India on 28.4.2000, HAI successfully evolved consensus among the Travel Agents Association of India (TAAI) and the Indian Association of Tour Operators (IATO) and the Hotel Association of India (HAI) resulting in the signing of the International Code of Practice governing the relations between Hoteliers, Travel Agents and Tour Operators.

The code represents a watershed for the tourism and travel industry in India, as protracted negotiations for adopting a code of practice for over three decades had not yielded any results till HAI took the lead and crafted consensus in favour of adopting the global practice.

It's signing by the three national bodies signalled to the international travel fraternity and business travellers that India had opted for internationally approved policies of hotel bookings, cancellations, refunds, claims etc.

The Legal 'First'

The Hotel Association of India took the lead in invoking the intervention of the High Court of Delhi in protecting the interests of hospitality industry in India on a matter of vital importance to the hotels as well as to the foreign and domestic tourist staying in hotels.

Hotel Association of India filed a writ in the High Court Delhi against an arbitrary and ad'hoc administrative directive requiring the hotels in approved categories, classified by the Ministry of Tourism, to follow a Single Tariff system.

The directive would have proved detrimental and counter productive to national tourism interests. The industry perspective presented by HAI was accepted by the High Court of Delhi which granted a Stay in favour of hotel industry, signifying an unique legal validation of hospitality industry system of operation across the country.

Seeking Repeal of Anti-women Legislation

The Punjab Excise Act enacted during the British rule in India in 1914 contains an archaic and anti-women provision prohibiting the employment of women in licenced premises, i.e., bars and restaurants in hotels. The Hotel Association of India challenged the validity of this ancient legislation before the Hon'ble High Court to protect the interest of women. The HAI's Writ against the constitutional validity of the provisions of the Punjab Excise Act, 1914

Media Centric Initiatives

The large number of foreign correspondents stationed in India, representing powerful and popular foreign publications, newspapers, journals, T. V. Channels, Broadcasters play a major role in making or marring the image of India as a peaceful tourists destination country through their news reports and dispatches. HAI took the lead in organizing the first ever hospitality industry meeting with the foreign correspondent stationed in New Delhi. The event was organized with the objective to discuss adverse the impact of Travel Advisories issued by foreign Governments on the State of Indian hospitality and tourism industry and correct their perspective to restore consumer confidence in travel, tourism and hospitality sectors adversely affected by global events of preceding years. Because of the unique nature of the special event and its potential for future tourists arrivals in India, the Ministry of Tourism fully associated with HAI.

Impact of Travel Advisories

Foreign Embassies and Missions are often instrumental in advising their respective countries to issue "Travel Advisories" to caution their citizens from undertaking visits to specific countries owing to adverse conditions of safety and security. Travel Advisories against visiting India were issued by several countries following global events like the terrorist attacks on 9/11 in USA and 13/12 in New Delhi,

War in Afghanistan and tension on Indo-Pak borders etc. The adverse travel advisories affected tourists arrivals to India over a prolonged period.

The Hotel Association of India stepped in by organizing an innovative Survey among foreign tourists staying in hotels to obtain their reactions to such advisories issued by the foreign governments. The HAI Survey brought out that a preponderant majority of tourists declared India as a safe and peaceful destination and foreign travellers viewed the travel advisories and warnings as "coloured by political considerations" and based on "inadequate knowledge of ground realities". Some of them opined that they found New Delhi "safer than Manhattan". HAI Survey facilitated the Governments of the respective countries in reviewing and withdrawing the adverse travel advisories and re-assured tourists of their safety and security in India.

Setting Up of Confederation of Indian Travel and Tourism Industry

Another first initiative mooted by the Association related to the need for creating a Confederation of Indian Travel and Tourism Industry (CITTI) as an umbrella organization to represent all components of the Travel & Travel industry in India. Unlike other industries, there has never been an umbrella organization in the tourism industry. To fill this gap, HAI proposed the setting up of CITTI which would address the policy issues and concerns of the industry. The Constitution of the proposed new body has been drawn up and made available to all sectoral associations to facilitate its establishment in the future.

TARIFF SYSTEM IN HOTELS

The first ever 'While Paper' on Tariff Systems in Hotels in India, produced by a Central Government Autonomous Organisation the National Institute of Public Finance and Policy (NIPFP), was undertaken at the behest of the Hotel

Association of India. The NIPFP headed by eminent economists of the standing of Dr. Raja J Chelliah, former Chief Economic Advisor of the Government of India and Dr. C. Rangarajan, former Governor of the Reserve Bank of India, provided the Indian hospitality industry with its most appropriate perspective and authentic study of tariff systems.

First Afro-Asian Infotech Hotels Expo

HAI-led initiative resulted in Afro-Asian Region's first Conference-cum-Exposition on Information Technology being institutionalized as 'an annual event in New Delhi for countries in the South Asian Region. The first Conference-cum-Expo organized by HAl on April 10-11, 2000 at the ITC Maurya Sheraton Hotel, New Delhi received support from the United Nations Economic and Social Commission for Asia and the Pacific, and the SAARC Tourism Council. The Ministries of Tourism and Information Technology, Government of India, extended official support to HAl as Co-sponsors of the event.

Second Afro-Asian Infotech Hotels Expo

The Second Conference-cum-Exposition on Information Technology in Hotels was organized on March 15-16, 2001 at the Taj Palace Hotel, New Delhi. This Afro-Asian conference was supported by United Nation Economic and Social Commission for Asia and like the front conference the Pacific (UN-ESCAP); Ministry of Tourism, Ministry of Information Technology, Government of India, SAARC Tourism Council and SAARC Hotel Association, Pacific Asia Travel Association (PATA) and International Hotel & Restaurant Association (IH&RA).

The HAI Chapters

The Hotel Association of India, established in April 1997, enlisted co-operation on a voluntary basis of professional hoteliers in twenty five State and fifty three cities to monitor hospitality related developments to enable the Association to address the concerns of the hospitality industry at the grass-roots level.

Going Global

Knowledge Exchange partnerships were formed with international organization such as the World Travel and Tourism Council (WTTC); the Pacific Asia Travel Association (PATA); World Tourism Organisation (WTO); the International Hotel and Restaurant Association (IH&RA); the United Nation Economic and Social Commission for Asia and the Pacific (UN-ESCAP); the South Asia Association of Regional Countries (SAARC), the World Health Organisation (WHO) and the European Union's South Asia Integrated Tourism Human Resource Development Programme (EU-SAITHRDP)

Inter-sectoral Linkages with Apex National Fora

At the National level working partnerships were established with apex industry for a like the Federation of Indian Chamber of Commerce and Industry (FICCI); Associated Chamber of Commerce and Industry of India (ASSOCHAM); Confederation of Indian Industry (CII); to provide hospitality industry perspective in the formation of national industrial policies and development.

Affiliation with WHO

HAI's pioneered the concept of 'Healthy Hotels' in line with WHO's 'Healthy Cities' campaign by initiating programmes for the hospitality industry on 'Hygiene Management in Hotels' at Agra in 1997. The WHO representative in India delivered the keynote address at the First Hygiene Management Seminar.

Innovative-"India Quiz Contest" at ITB Berlin 2002

A new promotional first was scored by the HAI at ITB Berlin, held from 16th to 20th March 2002. This was the first time 25 leading Indian hotels were brought together by HAI on the industry net to sponsor prizes of FAM Holiday Tours to Travel Trade visitors at the ITB.

The India Quiz Contest brochure of HAI provided a high visibility to the Indian hospitality industry products among visitor to the ITB, Berlin. The participating hotels received excellent marketing exposure of their properties in the Quiz brochure. This also offered unique opportunities for prospective agents and operator for the familiarization and experience of the hotels.

Disabled Friendly Facilities in Hotels

The Association undertook a pioneering role in formulating a comprehensive set of Guidelines for provision of Disabled Friendly facilities in Hotels, especially in parking and Approach Areas, Lobbies, Public Areas, Lifts, Rooms, Bathrooms and to install special Fire Prevention measures for the disabled.

Public-Private Partnership

The Association in a step towards promoting the public-private partnership called upon its members to extend their full corporation to the Archeological Survey of India in the maintenance of the National monuments, which has translated into following public-private sector partnership:-

(i) Illumination of Humayun's Tomb at Delhi by the Oberoi Group of Hotels.

(ii) Development of facilities for visitors at the Agra Fort by the ITC Hotels Ltd.

(iii) Main entrance of the Jantar Mantar observatory at New Delhi by the Apeejay Surrendra Park Hotels Pvt. Ltd.

(iv) Illumination of the Safdarjung Tomb, New Delhi by the Grand Group.

Special Promotional Packages

A major initiative undertaken by HAI galvanized the entire Indian hospitality industry to come together under the Association's banner to offer for the first time in the history of the industry as many as 62 special promotional packages in hotels for marketing averages in association with Air India.

Signing of MoU

The Hotel Association of India signed two Memorandum of Understanding which aimed at fostering and promoting tourism in their respective countries by inter alia agreeing to exchange information in respect to development and trend in the fields of tourism, hospitality and hotel sectors and encourage interaction between their respective hotels and Hospitality Association of India for Tourism Promotion and exploring investment opportunities in these sectors.

PATA Annual Conference

Encouraged by the overwhelming response received from the ITB Berlin, HAI launched its exclusive India Quiz Contest at the 51st PATA Annual Conference held in New Delhi from 14.04.2002 to 18.04.2002 offering opportunities of FAM Holiday in 14 leading Hotels.

Cross-cultural Tourists Movements in Hospitality Sector

HAI initiated a study project on Management of cross-cultural tourism movements in hospitality sector to assess and promote awareness among staff in smaller hotel and upgrade their knowledge and skills for handling of foreign tourists.

Fiscal Benefits Grants

For the first time the tourism industry's aspirations elaborated in the Hotel Association of India's various memoranda to the Central Government were translated into "tourism-friendly", measures in the Union Budget of 2003-04. These measures were aimed at making India more affordable destination, fuelling growth of hospitality infrastructure, facilitating business re-organisation, re-structuring hospitality industry and motivating State Governments to rationalize tourism tax regime. The major incentives extended to hospitality industries included and exemption of Service tax in hotels relating to Conference and Banquet business, which have been excluded from the service tax net.

Encouraging Investments

Hotel Association of India orchestrated the strategy leading to announcement in the Union Budget 2003 of benefits under Section 10(23) (g) on loans to hotels (3 star and above categories) for increasing the availability of funds for the hotel industry.

This provision has allowed lending institutions to make available funds to hotel projects at reduced rates of interest. The financial institutions will get a tax break on the interest income they earn on loans extended to such borrowers.

Inclusion of finance to the hotel projects of three star category and above for the first time under Section 10 (23)(g) of the Income Tax Act "signals" the positioning of hotels on the threshold of securing full infrastructure status as granted to other industries. HAI is now carrying this agenda forward to securing the wider benefits of infrastructure under Section 84 I/A of Income Tax Act.

Hospitality Business Restructuring

Amalgamation and Merger

It is at the behest of HAI that the Finance Ministry constituted a Working group under Chief Commissioner of Income Tax Mumbai which recommended the grant of benefits under Section 72 A of the Income Tax Act (which relates to the set-off of accumulated losses and depreciation on amalgamation), for the hotel industry to help loss-making hotel companies in re-organising their business.

The facility of mergers and acquisitions was hitherto available only to industrial undertakings and manufacturing units. With its extension to hotel companies, it has facilitated moves towards consolidation with the hospitality industry and releasing of resources blocked in non-performing assets.

This measure has now enabled smaller hotel units to enter into franchisee arrangements with established hotel groups/chains which in turn has led to improvements in occupancy levels and service standards.

Zero Duty Facility for Imports

HAI pursued with the Ministry of Commerce, Government of India for grant of the zero duty import facility to hotels and stand alone restaurants. The Industry has now been granted under the "Served from India Scheme", the zero duty facility to all hotels including one star, two star hotels for import of food items and alcoholic beverages sell which would make India an affordable destination.

HAI Directory

The exclusive HAI Directory of Hotels is an annual publication promoted with a singular aim of fulfilling the promotional need for tourists and visitor coming to India for an authentic compendium of leading Indian hotels recognized by the Ministry of Tourism. For the first time in 2005 the Directory was utilized by the Ministry of Tourism for distribution among foreign travel agents and tour operators in 12 countries through the Government of India's Tourist Offices abroad.

World Tourism Day

A new promotional first was scored by HAI for creating awareness about the World Tourism Day on 27th Sept. 2005 amongst not only the member-hotels but also the school children. To encourage and facilitate the member-hotels in celebrating the World Tourism Day on 27th September 2005, HAI outlined a bouquet of activities to be organized by the member-hotels. The member-hotels came forward in large numbers and organized the activities with enthusiasm and excitement. In New Delhi, HAI collaborated with the Sanskriti School to launch a Quiz Contest on Tourism for school children on the World Tourism Day.

Members Services

Variety of professional member-services are provided by HAI to its members these include:-

(i) INFORMATION BULLETINS sent out regularly with updates on latest developments concerning hotel industries, policy changes and pronouncements by Ministry of Tourism, Ministry of Finance, Ministry of Commerce, CBEC, CBDT, State Governments and affiliate international organizations such as WTTC, IH&RA, WTO etc.;

(ii) HAI TODAY-the first hospitality industry magazine of its kind in India;

(iii) HAI DIRECTORY OF HOTELS-an exclusive high quality reference manual of recognized hotels in India;

(iv) HAI PRIVILEGE CARDS which are offered to members in the Gold and Silver Categories entitling them to discounts on hotel room tariffs and restaurants outlets in all member hotels on reciprocal basis;

(v) HAI LEGAL SERVICES which enables members to avail benefits of highest calibre legal advice on issues of concern them and interventions on their behalf in courts.

HAI GREEN WEEKS

HAI has successfully institutionalized the concept of celebrating annual green weeks in hotels to exhibit its commitment to conservation of environment through use of bio-degradable and environment-friendly products by efficient management of waste generated and by adopting measures for efficient utilization of day light to conserve upon electricity etc. HAI has this year celebrated its ninth annual green week, reaching out to large number of tourists, employees, their families, school children and society with its environment message.

Fundamentals Of Revenue Management Will Be Revealed In A Special Report Commissioned By HSMAI Special Interest Group

MCLEAN, VA The Hospitality Sales & Marketing Association International (HSMAI) Revenue Management Special Interest Group has taken on an ambitious project to produce the first-ever comprehensive "Fundamentals of Revenue Management" special report.

The report will be a practitioner-friendly publication that addresses the fundamentals of revenue management for a broad audience of hospitality professionals. With comprehensive content that is both readable and actionable, it will deliver tools and information for revenue management education, incorporating expert advice from interviews with industry executives and educators, case studies, and practical checklists for implementing successful revenue management strategies at the property level.

"Creating relevance for members and the industry at large through ground-breaking initiatives such as this Revenue Management Special Report is in keeping with HSMAI's mission to be the leading source for sales and marketing information, knowledge and business development for professionals in tourism, travel, and hospitality," states Robert A. Gilbert, CHME, CHA, president and CEO of HSMAI.

"We are very excited about this debut project, and expect it will be a springboard for other initiatives including certification and revenue management research," notes Tim Wiersma, vice president of revenue management for Host Marriott and chair of HSMAI's Revenue Management Tangible Resources Committee.

The publication will be produced in a manner similar to the recent special report produced by HSMAI and TIG Global entitled DeMystifying Distribution, widely praised by the industry for its insight, accuracy and comprehensive coverage of the topic.

The commissioned report, which will be released at the third annual HSMAI Revenue Management Strategy Conference on June 19, 2005 in Minneapolis, will be co-authored by Caryl Helsel and Kathleen Cullen of the Solutionz Group, a business development and strategic consulting group based in Florida. Helsel heads the hospitality practice and previously held executive positions with Kimpton Hotels, Pegasus Solutions and Mandarin Oriental Hotel Group, and is the former president of the Hotel Electronic Distribution Network Association (HEDNA). Cullen is a lead consultant on the hospitality team and is a hospitality revenue management and distribution veteran, holding executive positions with Swissotel and Raffles Hotels, as well as past vice president of HEDNA. Delving deep into the fundamentals, nuances and specifics of revenue management, the special report will address the following:

- Ideas and initiatives to maximize revenue opportunities, optimize profits by managing revenues and develop an infrastructure (strategies, policies, procedures, reports, etc.) to make informed decisions about accepting or rejecting business.
- An overview of the external market such as segmentation, demand forecasting, revenue strategy, operational forecast, interdepartmental integration, strategic pricing, inventory control strategies and internal performance analysis.

- Tactics including rate-level maintenance, inventory management and rate offer assessment (for group and negotiated rates).
- The optimal environment, characteristics and descriptors.

The Revenue Management Special Interest Group is made up of a group of HSMAI members who advance the revenue management discipline through education, certification, participation, resources and guidance, enabling leaders to optimize revenue and performance within their own organizations. The SIG Advisory Board includes corporate revenue management executives from Accor North America, Destination Hotels & Resorts, Host Marriott Corporation, Hilton Hotels, InterContinental Hotels Group, Outrigger Hotels & Resorts, Peabody Hotels, Preferred Hotel Group, and TravelCLICK.

Among the Board's strategic intentions are:

- Provide education on all levels through programs, events, and an annual strategy conference as well as provide education for senior executives through publications, press releases and conference participation.
- Develop and manage a revenue management certification program.
- Develop a sense of community and participation.
- Provide tangible resources through a fundamentals publication that defines the discipline of revenue management and includes a glossary of terms, maintain a website portal, create a self-auditing system and encourage industry internships.

7

MANAGERS AND ASSISTANTS

JOB DESCRIPTION

A comfortable room, good food, and a helpful hotel staff can make being away from home an enjoyable experience for both vacationing families and business travellers. Hotel managers and assistant managers help their guests have a pleasant stay by providing many of the comforts of home, including cable television, fitness equipment, and voice mail.

Additionally, some hotels have health spas and other specialized services that the hotel manager and assistant help keep running smoothly. For business travellers, hotel managers often schedule available meeting rooms and electronic equipment, including slide projectors and fax machines. Hotel managers are responsible for keeping the operation of their establishments efficient and profitable.

In a small hotel, motel, or inn with a limited staff, the manager may oversee all aspects of operations. However, large hotels may employ hundreds of workers, and the general manager is usually aided by a number of assistant managers assigned to the various departments of the operation. In hotels of every size, managerial duties vary significantly by job title.

The general manager, for example, has overall responsibility for the operation of the hotel. Within guidelines established by the owners of the hotel or executives of the hotel chain, the general manager sets room rates, allocates funds to departments, approves expenditures, and establishes standards for service to guests, decor, housekeeping, food quality, and banquet operations. Managers who work for chains may also organize and staff a newly built hotel, refurbish an older hotel, or reorganize a hotel or motel that is not operating successfully. In order to fill some low-paying service and clerical jobs in hotels, some general managers attend career fairs. (For more information, see the statement on general managers and top executives elsewhere in the Handbook.)

Resident managers live in hotels and are on call 24 hours a day to resolve problems or emergencies. In general, though, they typically work an 8-hour day and oversee the day-to-day operations of the hotel. In many hotels, the general manager is also the resident manager.

Executive housekeepers ensure guest rooms, meeting and banquet rooms, and public areas are clean, orderly, and well maintained. They also train, schedule, and supervise the work of housekeepers, inspect rooms, and order cleaning supplies. Front office managers coordinate reservations and room assignments as well as train and direct the hotel's front desk staff. They ensure that guests are treated courteously, complaints and problems are resolved, and requests for special services are carried out. Front office managers often have authorization to adjust charges posted on a customer's bill.

Food and beverage managers direct the food service operations of hotels. They oversee the hotels' restaurants, cocktail lounges, and banquet facilities. These managers also supervise food and beverage preparation and service workers, plan menus, set schedules, estimate costs, and deal with food suppliers.

Convention services managers coordinate the activities of large hotels' various departments for meetings, conventions, and special events. They meet with representatives of groups or organizations to plan the number of rooms to reserve, the desired configuration of hotel meeting space, and the banquet services. During the meeting or event, they resolve unexpected problems and monitor activities to ensure that hotel operations conform to the expectations of the group.

Assistant managers help run the day-to-day operations of the hotel. In large hotels they may be responsible for activities such as personnel, accounting, office administration, marketing and sales, purchasing, security, maintenance, and pool, spa, or recreational facilities. In smaller hotels, these duties may be combined into one position. Some hotels allow an assistant manager to make decisions regarding hotel guest charges when a manager is unavailable.

Computers are used extensively by hotel managers and their assistants to keep track of the guest's bill, reservations, room assignments, meetings, and special events. In addition, computers are used to order food, beverages, and supplies, as well as to prepare reports for hotel owners and top-level managers. Managers work with computer specialists to ensure that the hotel's computer system functions properly. Should the hotel's computer system fail, managers must continue to meet guests' needs.

CONDITIONS OF WORK

Because hotels are open around the clock, night and weekend work is common. Many hotel managers work more than 40 hours per week. Managers who live in the hotel usually have regular work schedules, but they may be called to work at any time. Some employees of resort hotels are managers during the busy season and have other duties during the rest of the year.

Hotel managers sometimes experience the pressures of coordinating a wide range of functions. Conventions and large groups of tourists may present unusual problems.

Moreover, dealing with irate guests can be stressful. The job can be particularly hectic for front office managers during check-in and check-out time. Computer failures can further complicate an already busy time.

EMPLOYMENT

Hotel managers and assistant managers held about 76,000 jobs in 1998. Self-employed managers-primarily owners of small hotels and motels-held a significant number of these jobs. Companies that manage hotels and motels under contract employed some managers.

TRAINING

Hotels increasingly emphasize specialized training. Postsecondary training in hotel or restaurant management is preferred for most hotel management positions, although a college liberal arts degree may be sufficient when coupled with related hotel experience. Internships or part-time or summer work is an asset to students seeking a career in hotel management. The experience gained and the contacts made with employers can greatly benefit them after graduation. Most bachelor's degree programs include work-study opportunities.

In the past, many managers were promoted from the ranks of front desk clerks, housekeepers, waiters and chefs, and hotel sales workers. Although some employees still advance to hotel management positions without education beyond high school, postsecondary education is preferred. Restaurant management training or experience is also a good background for entering hotel management because the success of a hotel's food service and beverage operations is often of great importance to the profitability of the entire establishment.

In 1998, nearly 200 community and junior colleges and some universities offered associate, bachelor's, and graduate degree programs in hotel or restaurant management. When combined with technical institutes, vocational and trade schools, and other academic institutions, over 800 educational facilities have programs leading to formal recognition in hotel or restaurant management. Hotel management programs include instruction in hotel administration, accounting, economics, marketing, housekeeping, food service management and catering, and hotel maintenance engineering. Computer training is also an integral part of hotel management training due to the widespread use of computers in reservations, billing, and housekeeping management.

Hotel managers must be able to get along with many different people, even in stressful situations. They must be able to solve problems and concentrate on details. Initiative, self-discipline, effective communication skills, and the ability to organize and direct the work of others are also essential for managers at all levels.

Most hotels promote employees who have proven their ability and completed formal education in hotel management. Graduates of hotel or restaurant management programs usually start as trainee assistant managers. Some large hotels sponsor specialized on-the-job management training programs allowing trainees to rotate among various departments and gain a thorough knowledge of the hotel's operation. Other hotels may help finance formal training in hotel management for outstanding employees. Newly built hotels, particularly those without well-established on-the-job training programs, often prefer experienced personnel for managerial positions.

Large hotel and motel chains may offer better opportunities for advancement than small, independently owned establishments, but relocation every several years often is necessary for advancement. The large chains have more extensive career ladder programs and offer managers the opportunity to transfer to another hotel or motel in the chain or to the central office. Career advancement can be accelerated by completion of certification programs offered by the associations listed below. These programs usually require a combination of course work, examinations, and experience.

OUTLOOK

Employment of hotel managers and assistants is expected to grow more slowly than the average for all occupations through 2008. Long hours and stressful working conditions result in high turnover in this field, so additional job openings are expected to occur as experienced managers transfer to other occupations, retire, or stop working for other reasons. Job opportunities in hotel management are expected to be especially good for persons with college degrees in hotel or restaurant management.

Increasing business travel and domestic and foreign tourism will drive employment growth of hotel managers and assistants. Managerial jobs are not expected to grow as rapidly as the hotel industry overall, however. As the industry consolidates, many chains and franchises will acquire independently owned establishments and increase the number of economy-class rooms to accommodate bargain-conscious guests. Economy hotels offer clean, comfortable rooms and front desk services without costly extras like restaurants and room service. Because there are not as many departments in these hotels, fewer managers will be needed. In addition, front desk clerks are increasingly assuming some responsibilities previously reserved for managers, further limiting the growth of managers and their assistants.

Additional demand for managers, however, is expected in suite hotels as some guests, especially business customers, are willing to pay higher prices for rooms with kitchens and suites that provide the space needed to conduct meetings. In addition to job growth in suite hotels and economy-class hotels, large full-service hotels-offering restaurants, fitness centers, large meeting rooms, and play areas for children, among other amenities-will continue to offer many trainee and managerial opportunities.

SALARY

Median annual earnings of hotel managers and assistants were $26,700 in 1998. The middle 50 percent of these workers earned between $19,820 and $34,690. The lowest 10 percent had earnings of less than $14,430, while the top 10 percent earned over $45,520. In 1997, median annual earnings in the hotel and other lodging places industry, where nearly all of these workers are employed, were $28,600.

Salaries of hotel managers and assistants vary greatly according to their responsibilities and the segment of the hotel industry in which they are employed. Managers may earn bonuses up to 25 percent of their basic salary in some hotels and may also be furnished with lodging, meals, parking, laundry, and other services. In addition to typical benefits, some hotels offer profit-sharing plans and educational assistance to their employees.

8

LOCATION OF THE HOTEL

Location is one of the most important factors in choosing a hotel. Whether they travel for business or pleasure, people need a place to stay when they are away from home. Some very special hotels-New York's Waldorf-Astoria or San Francisco's Ritz-Carlton, for example-become destinations in themselves.

But most travellers know where they want to go and then select a hotel that fits their needs. Many travellers prefer to stay at "branded" hotels-places that offer the familiarity of well-known franchises in both accommodations and food services regardless of the location. Other travellers believe that branded hotels lack uniqueness and seek out smaller, independent hotels when they travel. Hotel locations are closely linked to transportation. America's earliest hotels were small public inns that catered to passengers who arrived in horse-drawn wagons. They were built along major roads and at river crossings. Then railroads built a travel network across the country, and new, larger hotels sprang up near the main stations.

HOSPITALITY AND RECREATION

The travel and tourism industry is by its very nature global in scope. By the beginning of the twenty-first century, however, travel destinations and vacation activities were changing. Perhaps the hottest trend in travel is the rise of "ecotourism." According to the Quebec Declaration on

Ecotourism, ecotourism "includes local and indigenous communities in its planning, interprets the natural and cultural heritage of the destination to the visitor, and lends itself better to independent travellers."

Not so long ago many of the now-popular ecotourism destinations were either unknown to the outside world or fairly inaccessible. For most people places such as the Amazon rain forest, Africa's savannas, and the Himalaya and Andes mountains were simply out of reach. But many countries are now promoting their remote environmental treasures to travellers looking for something out of the ordinary. Tour operators are developing special packages for the environmentally minded traveler, and local groups are organizing tourism associations that attract tourists to out-of-the-way places.

Archaeological tourism is another growing trend. Ancient sites in destinations such as Egypt, Israel, and various other places in the Middle East are attracting visitors who only a short time ago had little knowledge of that region of the world. In 2005 Archaeological Tours in New York City offered packages that allowed travellers to explore the ancient Silk Road of China, the Byzantine monuments in southern Italy, and the legendary statues of Easter Island. Most of the tours were led by archeologists or university professors.

The development of ecotourism and archaeological tourism has coincided with an increase in travel to the United States by foreign tourists. Along with a global economy has come a growing middle class in Asia and Latin America. Latin America's outbound travel market has grown almost 33 percent since the mid-1990s, according to a 2004 online article by the Travel Industry Association of America. A good number of these newly prosperous travellers will eventually make their way to the United States.

Another travel trend has its roots in America's history as a country of immigrants. In recent years many Americans have begun searching for relatives or ancestors both at home and abroad. As distant parts of the world grow closer together, travellers are finding more opportunities for what has come to be called "heritage travel" to Europe, Asia, Africa, and Central and South America.

No innovation has affected the hotel industry more than the automobile. With the invention of the automobile, locations throughout the country became far more accessible to travellers. Motels, or "motor hotels," were built to accommodate drivers as they explored America. Early motels were usually small, family-owned businesses with a few roadside cabins. Air travel has further expanded the possible locations to which people can travel. Moreover, the Internet has had a profound impact on tourism. Potential travellers can explore vacation packages and make reservations online. According to a 2005 article published in Revenue, travel researcher PhoCusWright noted that half of flight and hotel reservations were made online by the end of 2005.

THE HOTEL INDUSTRY TRENDS

In the first five years of the twentieth century hotel chains dominated the industry. In 2000 chains controlled nearly 70 percent of the hotel market share in the United States while less than 40 percent of all hotels were independently owned and operated. Just ten years earlier in 1990 nearly 55 percent of all hotels were independent.

Hotel chains have flourished because they offer consumers a reliable and predictable visit. Each hotel in a chain offers similar facilities and services. Many are adding services from nationally known franchises such as pizzerias or Starbucks coffee shops. This similarity makes them popular because travellers going to an unfamiliar city know what to expect if they have stayed in another hotel or motel in the same chain.

The hotel industry faces fierce competition due to an oversupply of hotel rooms. A construction boom in the 1980s was followed by a decline in the number of travellers during the early 1990s. Hotel occupancy fell from a high of 72 percent in 1979 to just 59.2 percent in 2003, leaving more than one-third of all hotel rooms empty on any given night. The result of this oversupply has been increased market segmentation. Rather than running huge, five-hundred-room hotels to fit the needs of every traveler, many hotels today target one market segment such as business or budget travellers.

Some innovative hotel designs have also captured markets successfully. One popular trend has been the all-suite hotel. Each unit in an all-suite hotel provides a living area and a separate bedroom.

Some also offer a cooking area. Another development is the environmentally conscious "ecohotel," which highlights features such as low-flush toilets, refillable containers for toiletries, and recycled stationery. One of the most popular promotions in resort locations is the all-inclusive package, which offers travellers not only lodging but all meals, drinks, and entertainment for one price.

The growth of the global economy has also affected the hotel industry. Many hotel chains based in the United States have expanded overseas. At home the hotel industry made a slow recovery from 9/11 but was still coping with the effects of the recession through the first decade of the new century. According to a March 2005 report in the Fairfield County Business Journal, the typical U.S. hotel achieved an estimated 13.3 percent increase in yearly profits in 2004. Moreover, an increased confidence in airport security, a decreased fear of a terrorist attack, and a weak U.S. dollar has led to an increase in foreign travel to the United States. During the first half of 2004 international spending in America rose for the first time since 9/11.

In 2004 the U.S. Commerce Department estimated that foreign tourism accounted for over $71 billion in economic activity in the United States-a figure larger than the profits from U.S. automobile, engine, and parts exports. With that much at stake, it is little surprise that President George W. Bush approved a $50 million ad campaign aimed at tourists in England, Japan, Germany, Canada, and Mexico.

Hotels make foreign travellers feel welcome by serving international cuisine in their restaurants and by providing room directories and menus printed in several languages. Some hotels now employ multilingual concierges to help guests with making reservations, arranging tours, and answering questions about the region. This trend increases the demand for workers who speak several languages and who have experience with different cultures. In April 2005 Wyndham Hotels announced it would implement an English language education program for its Spanish-speaking employees.

Business Travellers

One major market segment for the hotel industry is business travel. Hotels in all price ranges compete to attract these guests and keep them as clients. Employees who have sales and marketing experience can help a hotel compete successfully.

Hotels seek business travellers by providing special features or services designed to make it easier to work away from home. During the 1980s many hotels built business centers that included computers and copiers. Portable technology has lessened the popularity of these centers, and now many business travellers prefer to work in their rooms using their own notebook computers. By the early 2000s popular hotel amenities included free newspapers, a complimentary breakfast, a large work desk, high-speed or WiFi Internet access, and exercise facilities.

Efficiency is a primary concern for all business travellers whose tight schedules require quick service. Many hotels provide computerized services for speedy check-in and check-out. Employees are trained to help visits run smoothly and to handle problems swiftly. As in any service industry, pleasing the customer is of foremost importance.

Some business-oriented hotels offer facilities for companies to conduct extended staff meetings. It is also common for businesses to schedule "retreats" where employees stay at the same hotel and discuss business strategies in designated meeting rooms, then spend time together participating in leisure activities such as golf, tennis, or swimming. Many hotels are designed to cater to these meetings, especially those at popular resort destinations.

Earning customer loyalty is a key feature of serving business travellers. If a hotel satisfies a business client, the long-term return can be great. One way that hotels promote customer loyalty is through frequent-guest programs. Travellers earn points for every dollar they spend at the hotel. When they have accumulated enough points, they can redeem them for gifts such as free lodging or a vacation at an exotic resort.

Like all aspects of the hospitality industry, business and convention travel was hit hard by 9/11 and the sagging economy. From 1998 to 2003, business and convention travel experienced a 14 percent drop-off; however, business travel grew more than 4 percent in 2004 and should experience even more growth in the next few years, according to the Travel Industry Association of America.

CONVENTIONS

Guest rooms are only one source of revenue for many hotels. They can make large profits by renting meeting rooms and exhibition space and by hosting banquets and receptions. Trade shows and conventions draw hundreds of customers at a time to a hotel.

Many different industries and business organizations hold trade shows and conventions each year. Political, civic, religious, and social organizations also have annual meetings. Hotels hire convention planners to attract conventions, to help businesses plan events, and to negotiate prices. During a convention service managers supervise every stage of the event. Because a hotel's reputation for efficiency and good service is often the key to its success in attracting conventions, the work of the convention staff is critical.

TERMS OF HOTEL WORKERS

The workers in a large hotel generally are organized into teams according to the department in which they work. There are currently more than 170 different careers in the hospitality industry. Common departments include sales, food and beverage, housekeeping, and accounting. Each department is run by a manager, who usually reports to a general manager in charge of the hotel.

Hotel workers are traditionally described as "front-of-the-house" or "back-of-the-house" employees, depending on whether they have direct contact with the guests. Front-of-the-house workers include bellhops, desk clerks, and concierges. Back-of-the-house workers are the behind-the-scenes employees who keep the hotel running smoothly. They include kitchen workers, housekeepers, and accountants.

THE FOOD SERVICE

Any business that prepares and serves meals, snacks, or beverages is part of the food service industry. The largest segment of the industry includes restaurants serving full menus and offering table service. The second-largest segment is limited-menu, or fast food, outlets. Although large fast food chains are a familiar sight all across the United States, more than seven out of ten eating and drinking places are single-unit, independent operations. Other segments of the food service industry include school and employee cafeterias, catering businesses, hotel restaurants, and vendors at sporting events and concerts. The food service industry in the United States is booming and appears to be immune from the weak economy of the twenty-first century's first decade. Sales have increased from about $43 billion in 1970 to $426 billion in 2003. The National Restaurant Association estimates that more than 54 billion meals were eaten in restaurants and school and work cafeterias in 2002. Social scientists suggest that the boom is the result of people's busy schedules. They also point out that dual-income families have limited time for cooking. Although the rapid food service boom of the 1970s and 1980s may be slowing, the employment outlook is still very good. In 2002 the food service industry employed about 11.7 million workers, making it the largest U.S. employer besides the government. Food and beverage service employment is expected to reach 13.3 million by 2012.

Recent Trends

The growth of the take-out food market is a major trend in the food service industry. This market segment is called the "off-premises sector" because food is eaten away from the restaurant where it is cooked. It includes take-out, delivery, and drive-through restaurants. Many traditional restaurants that offer table service attempt to cash in on this expanding market by offering delivery service. Take-out and delivery accounted for 51 percent of total restaurant business in 2002. The Internet has also had a profound influence on the food service market; many workers now order their lunches online.

After rapid expansion in the 1980s the number of fast food restaurants remained stable through the 1990s. New restaurants are likely to be full-service restaurants, which cater more successfully to America's older population. In fact, the full-service sector is expected to be the fastest-growing sector in the industry The number of Americans between the ages of fifteen and thirty-four-the age group that generally thrives on fast food-is decreasing, whereas the food service industry includes any business that prepares and serves meals, snacks, or beverages. Number of Americans age sixty-five or older is increasing. Many older diners have more time for a leisurely meal and do not seek out fast food.

Like any other business, fast food restaurants must adapt to changing times. Many fast-food chains are offering a wider range of choices and emphasizing low-fat items such as salads and grilled foods to appeal to health-conscious Americans. Another significant trend is the growth of the ethnic food sector. Whereas many Americans once limited their exploration of ethnic foods to Italian or Chinese cuisine, today they seek out traditional foods of Latin America, India, Africa, the Caribbean, and other cultures.

The Food Service Workers

The people who work in the food service industry include food and beverage managers, restaurant managers, bartenders, chefs and cooks, bakers, dining room and cafeteria attendants, hostesses and hosts, waiters and waitresses, fast food franchise workers, caterers, stewards, dishwashers, and other kitchen workers. The food service industry employs large numbers of relatively unskilled workers. Restaurants traditionally have depended on young people to fill these positions; however, low birthrates in the 1970s and 1980s limited the number of youths looking for employment in the 1990s. The food service industry was forced to attract workers from other age groups. It became common for food service businesses to offer more full-time employment, higher wages and bonuses, and more training for career advancement than before. The industry also began recruiting more women and minorities, as well as nontraditional workers such as seniors and mentally and physically challenged individuals.

9

PROCESS AND TECHNIQUES OF ORGANIZING

SUPERVISION

A key issue in accomplishing the goals identified in the planning process is structuring the work of the organization. Organizations are groups of people, with ideas and resources, working toward common goals. The purpose of the organizing function is to make the best use of the organization's resources to achieve organizational goals. Organizational structure is the formal decision-making framework by which job tasks are divided, grouped, and coordinated. Formalization is an important aspect of structure.

It is the extent to which the units of the organization are explicitly defined and its policies, procedures, and goals are clearly stated. It is the official organizational structure conceived and built by top management. The formal organization can be seen and represented in chart form. An organization chart displays the organizational structure and shows job titles, lines of authority, and relationships between departments.

The informal organization is the network, unrelated to the firm's formal authority structure, of social interactions among its employees. It is the personal and social relationships that arise spontaneously as people associate with one another in the work environment. The supervisor must realize that the informal organization affects the formal ...nization. The informal organization can pressure group members to conform to the expectations of the informal group that conflict with those of the formal organization. This can result in the generation of false information or rumours and resistance to change desired by management. The supervisor should recognize the existence of information groups, identify the roles member play within these groups, and use knowledge of the groups to work effectively with them. The informal organization can make the formal organization more effective by providing support to management, stability to the environment, and useful communication channels.

THE ORGANIZATIONAL STRUCTURE

Even though the differences among organizations are enormous, there are many similarities that enable them to be classified. One widely used classification is the twofold system (mechanistic versus organic forms of organizational structure) developed by Tom Burns and G. M. Stalker in their study of electronics firms in the United Kingdom.

The mechanistic structure is the traditional or classical design, common in many medium-and large-size organizations. Mechanistic organizations are somewhat rigid in that they consist of very clearly delineated jobs, have a well-defined hierarchical structure, and rely heavily on the formal chain of command for control. Bureaucratic organizations, with their emphasis on formalization, are the primary form of mechanistic structures. According to Max Weber, bureaucracy is a form of organization characterized by a rational, goal-directed hierarchy, impersonal decision making, formal controls, and subdivision into managerial positions and specialization of labour. Bureaucratic organizations are tall consisting of hierarchies with many levels of management. In a tall structure, people become relatively confined to their own area of specialization. Bureaucracies are driven by a top-down or command and control approach in which managers provide considerable direction and have considerable control over others. Other features of the bureaucratic organization include functional division of labour and work specialization.

On the other hand, the organic structure is more flexible, more adaptable to a participative form of management, and less concerned with a clearly defined structure. The organic organization is open to the environment in order to capitalize upon new opportunities.

Organic organizations have a flat structure with only one or two levels of management. Flat organizations emphasize a decentralized approach to management that encourage high employee involvement in decisions. The purpose of this structure is to create independent small businesses or enterprises that can rapidly respond to customers' needs or changes in the business environment. The supervisor tends to have a more personal relationship with his or her employees.

Rensis Likert has conducted extensive research on a non-bureaucratic organization design referred to as System 4 (participative-democratic). Management and employees interact in a friendly environment characterized by mutual confidence and trust.

Contingency organization means that the most appropriate organization structure for each situation depends upon technology, organizational size, goals and strategy, environmental stability, and characteristics of the employees. Mechanistic organizations are best suited to repetitive operations and stable environments, while organic organizations are best suited to an uncertain task and a changing environment.

DESIGN

Designing an organization involves choosing an organizational structure that will enable the company to ... effectively achieve its goals. Organization design is the creation of an organization's structure, traditionally functional, divisional, and/or matrix.

Functions or divisions arrange traditional organizations. In a functional organization, authority is determined by the relationships between group functions and activities. Functional structures group similar or related occupational specialties or processes together under the familiar headings of finance, manufacturing, marketing, accounts receivable, research, surgery, and photo finishing. Economy is achieved through specialization. However, the organization risks losing sight of its overall interests as different departments pursue their own goals. In a divisional organization, corporate divisions operate as relatively autonomous businesses under the larger corporate umbrella. In a conglomerate organization, divisions may be unrelated. Divisional structures are made up of self-contained strategic business units that each produces a single product. For example, General Motors' divisions include Chevrolet, Oldsmobile, Pontiac, and Cadillac. A central headquarters, focusing or results, coordinates and controls the activities, and provides support services between divisions. Functional departments accomplish division goals. A weakness however, is the tendency to duplicate activities among divisions.

In a matrix organization, teams are formed and team members report to two or more managers. Matrix structures utilize functional and divisional chains of command simultaneously in the same part of the organization, commonly for one-of-a-kind projects. It is used to develop a new product, to ensure the continuing success of a product to which several departments directly contribute, and to solve a difficult problem. By superimposing a project structure upon the functional structure, a matrix organization is formed that allows the organization to take advantage of new opportunities. This structure assigns specialists from different functional departments to work on one or more projects being led by project managers. The matrix concept facilitates working on concurrent projects by creating a dual chain of command, the project (program, systems, or product) manager and the functional manager. Project managers have authority over activities geared toward achieving organizational goals while functional managers have authority over promotion decisions and performance reviews. An example is an aerospace firm with a contract from NASA.

Matrix organizations are particularly appealing to firms that want to speed up the decision-making process. However, the matrix organization may not allow long-term working relationships to develop. Furthermore, using multiple managers for one employee may result in confusion as to manager evaluation and accountability. Thus, the matrix system may elevate the conflict between product and functional interests.

Boundaryless organizations are not defined or limited by horizontal, vertical, or external boundaries imposed by a predetermined structure. They share many of the characteristics of flat organizations, with a strong emphasis on teams. Cross-functional teams dissolve horizontal barriers and enable the organization to respond quickly to environmental changes and to spearhead innovation. Boundaryless organizations can form relationships (joint ventures, intellectual property, distribution channels, or financial resources) with customers, suppliers, and/or competitors. Telecommuting, strategic alliances and customer-organization linkages break down external barriers, streamlining work activities. Jack Welch, former CEO of General Electric, to facilitate interactions with customers and suppliers, first used this un-structure.

A boundaryless environment is required by learning organizations to facilitate team collaboration and the sharing of information. When an organization develops the continuous capacity to adapt and survive in an increasingly competitive ...vironment because all members take an active role in ... resolving work-related issues, it has developed a learning culture. A learning organization is one that is able to adapt and respond to change. This design empowers employees because they acquire and share knowledge and apply this learning to decision-making. They are pooling collective intelligence and stimulating creative thought to improve performance. Supervisors facilitate learning by sharing and aligning the organization's vision for the future and sustaining a sense of community and strong culture.

FUNCTION OF ORGANISING

The organizing function deals with all those activities that result in the formal assignment of tasks and authority and a coordination of effort. The supervisor staffs the work unit, trains employees, secures resources, and empowers the work group into a productive team. The steps in the organizing process include (1) review plans, (2) list all tasks to be accomplished, (3) divide tasks into groups one person can accomplish-a job, (4) group related jobs together in a logical and efficient manner, (5) assign work to individuals, (6) delegate authority to establish relationships between jobs and groups of jobs.

The nature and scope of the work needed to accomplish the organization's objectives is needed to determine work classification and work unit design. Division of labour, or work specialization, is the degree to which tasks in an organization are divided into separate jobs. Work process requirements and employee skill level determine the degree of specialization. Placing capable people in each job ties directly with productivity improvement. In order to maximize productivity, supervisors match employee skill level with task requirements.

Supervisors should perform workflow analysis to examine how work creates or adds value to the ongoing processes in an organization. Workflow analysis looks at how work moves from the customer or the demand source through the organization to the point at which the work leaves the organization as a product or service to meet customer demand. Thus, workflow analysis can be used to tighten the connection between employees' work and customers' needs. Also, it can help to make major performance breakthroughs throughout business process reengineering (BPR), a fundamental rethinking and radical redesign of business processes to achieve dramatic improvements in costs, quality, service, and speed. BPR uses workflow analysis to identify jobs that can be eliminated or recombined to improve company performance.

DEPARTMENTALIZATION

After reviewing the plans, usually the first step in the organizing process is departmentalization. Once jobs have been classified through work specialization, they are grouped so those common tasks can be coordinated. Departmentalization is the basis on which work or individuals are grouped into manageable units. There are five traditional methods for grouping work activities.

- Departmentalization by function organizes by the functions to be performed. The functions reflect the nature of the business. The advantage of this type of grouping is obtaining efficiencies from consolidating similar specialties and people with common skills, knowledge and orientations together in common units.
- Departmentalization by product assembles all functions needed to make and market a particular product are placed under one executive. For instance, major department stores are structured around product groups such as home accessories, appliances, women's clothing, men's clothing, and children's clothing.
- Departmentalization by geographical regions groups jobs on the basis of territory or geography. For example, Merck, a major pharmaceutical company,

has its domestic sales departmentalized by regions such as Northeast, Southeast, Midwest, Southwest, and Northwest.

- Departmentalization by process groups jobs on the basis of product or customer flow. Each process requires particular skills and offers a basis for homogeneous categorizing of work activities. A patient preparing for an operation would first engage in preliminary diagnostic tests, then go through the admitting process, undergo a procedure in surgery, receive post operative care, be discharged and perhaps receive out-patient attention. These services are each administered by different departments.
- Departmentalization by customer groups jobs on the basis of a common set of needs or problems of specific customers. For instance, a plumbing firm may group its work according to whether it is serving private sector, public sector, government, or not-for-profit organizations. A current departmentalization trend is to structure work according to customer, using cross-functional teams. This group is chosen from different functions to work together across various departments to interdependently create new products or services. For example, a cross-functional team consisting of managers from accounting, finance, and marketing is created to prepare a technology plan.

AUTHORITY AND POWER

Organizational structure is a means of facilitating the achievement of organizational objectives. Such structures are not static, but dynamic. They reorganize in response to changing conditions that occur in the environment, new technology, or organizational growth. Organization structures are dependent upon the employees whose activities they guide. Supervisors rely upon power and authority to ensure that employees get things done.

Authority

The organizational structure provides the framework for the formal distribution of authority. Formalization is the degree to which tasks are standardized and rules and regulations govern employee behavior. It influences the amount of discretion an employee has over his or her job. In an organization with high degrees of formalization, job descriptions and policies provide clear direction. Where formalization is low, employees have a great deal of freedom in deciding how thy conduct their work. Within the same organization, different departments may have different degrees of formalization. For example, in a hospital, doctors have freedom in selecting treatments, drugs, and methods for treating patients. However, the hospital physical plant staff has a strict schedule for cleaning buildings, mowing lawns, and maintaining the facilities.

Authority is the legitimate power of a supervisor to direct subordinates to take action within the scope of the supervisor's position. Formal authority in the organization can be traced all the way back to the U.S. constitutional right to own property. The owner of the organization has the authority to make decisions. For example, entrepreneurial firms have an informal arrangement of employees and centralization of decision-making authority, the owner.

Forms of Authority

Three forms of authority are line authority, staff authority, and team authority.

Line authority is direct supervisory authority from superior to subordinate. Authority flows in a direct chain of command from the top of the company to the bottom. Chain of command is an unbroken line of reporting relationships that extends through the entire organization that defines the formal decision-making structure. It helps employees know to whom they are accountable, and whom to go to with a problem. Line departments are directly linked to the production and sales of specific products. Supervisors--in line departments, such as marketing and production--give direct orders, evaluate performance, and reward or punish those employees who work for them. Unity of command within the chain states that each person in an organization should take orders from and reports to only one person. This helps prevent conflicting demands being placed on employees by more than one boss.

However, the trend toward employee empowerment, fuelled by advances in technology and changes in design from downsizing and reengineering have tempered the importance of being accountable to only one superior. Span of control refers to the number of employees that should be placed under the direction of one manager. Spans within effective organizations vary greatly. The actual number depends on the amount of complexity and the level of specialization. In general, a wide span of control is possible with better-trained, more experienced, and committed employees.

Staff authority is more limited authority to advise. It is authority that is based on expertise and which usually involves advising line managers. Staff members are advisers and counselors who aid line departments in making decisions but do not have the authority to make final decisions. Staff supervisors help line departments decide what to do and how to do it. They coordinate and provide technical assistance or advice to all advisors, such as accounting, human resources, information technology, research, advertising, public relations, and legal services.

Team authority is granted to committees or work teams involved in an organization's daily operations. Work teams are groups of operating employees empowered to plan and organize their own work and to perform that work with a minimum of supervision. Team-Based structures organize separate functions into a group based on one overall objective. Empowered employees create their own schedules, design their own processes, and are held responsible for outcomes. This facilitates efficiencies in work process, and the ability to detect and react to changes in the environment. Employees with the skills and knowledge to manage more than one specialized task are able to promptly provide customers with quality products and services. Cross-functionally training team members allows any member to perform a variety of problem-solving tasks.

Teamwork is an imperative in a flat, boundaryless organizational structure. A team is a small number of people with complementary skills who work toward common goals for which they hold themselves mutually accountable. Self-managed teams are responsible for producing an entire product, a component, or an ongoing service. In most cases, members are cross-trained on the different tasks assigned to the team. Often, these teams are trained in technical, administrative, and interpersonal skills. Problem-solving teams do not affect an organization's structure because they exist for only a limited period.

They are often used when organizations decide to make improvements in the quality of a product or service. Special-purpose teams consist of members who span functional or organizational boundaries and whose purpose is to examine complex issues such as introducing new technology, improving the quality of work process, or encouraging cooperation between labour and management in a unionized setting.

Power

In addition to authority, supervisors have more personal sources of power to draw upon for getting things done. Everyone has power in one form or another and it is by exercising this power that organizations get things accomplished. Supervisors who are capable of achieving their objectives independently of others are said to possess strength. When these "strong" supervisors involve and incorporate others into their plans and activities they are making use of power, and in fact increasing the total amount of power available to incorporate into a particular situation or problem. Involving employees in setting objectives and making decisions as it relates to their jobs empowers everyone, and results in greater job satisfaction and commitment, as well as increased productivity. Empowering employees provides them with greater autonomy.

Power is the ability to exert influence in the organization beyond authority, which is derived from position. The supervisor's personal power could include job knowledge, personal influence, interpersonal skills, and ability to get results, empathetic ability, persuasive ability, and physical strength. J.P. French and B. Raven ("The Bases of Social Power" in Studies in Social Power, edited by D. Cartwright, Institute for Social Research, 1959, pp. 150-167) identify six sources of power: legitimate, coercive, reward, expert, referent, and information. Legitimate power is a result of the position a person holds in the organization hierarchy. This position power is broader than the ability to reward and punish, as members need to accept the authority of the position.

Coercive power is the threat of sanctions. It is dependent on fear and includes, but is not limited to the ability to dismiss, assign undesirable work, or restriction of movement. Reward power results in people doing what is asked because they desire positive benefits or rewards. Rewards can be anything a person values (praise, raises, and promotions). Expert power comes from expertise, skill, or knowledge. Referent power refers to a person who has desirable resources or personal traits. It results in admiration and the desire to emulate. Information power is based upon the persuasiveness or content of a communication and is independent of the influencing individual.

In most instances, supervisors do not need to offer incentives or threaten retribution to get employees to do what they request. They influence employees because the employees want to follow. This power to influence comes from the employee granting authority to the supervisor.

CENTRALIZATION AND DECENTRALIZATION

Centralization is the degree to which decision-making is concentrated in top management's hands. Decentralization is the extent to which decision-making authority is pushed down the organization structure and shared with many lower-level employees. Centralized organizations have more levels of management with narrow spans of control. Employees are not free to make decisions. Decentralized organizations have fewer levels of management with wide spans of control giving employees more freedom of action. All other things being equal, a wide span of control is more efficient because it requires fewer managers. However, it is important to recognize that, at some point, effectiveness will decline.

The current trend is toward broadening decentralization. As competition intensifies, the need for organizations to be responsive increases. This has made employees, usually those at the lower levels, who are closest to customers extremely important. They are an excellent source of knowledge and implement changes that directly impact performance. Giving this group more input into certain decision-making activities can result in increased firm performance.

It is impractical for the supervisor to handle all of the work of the department directly. In order to meet the organization's goals, focus on objectives, and ensure that all work is accomplished, supervisors must delegate authority. Authority is the legitimate power of a supervisor to direct subordinates to take action within the scope of the supervisor's position. By extension, this power, or a part thereof, is delegated and used in the name of a supervisor. Delegation is the downward transfer of formal authority from superior to subordinate. The employee is empowered to act for the supervisor, while the supervisor remains accountable for the outcome. Delegation of authority is a person-to-person relationship requiring trust, commitment, and contracting between the supervisor and the employee.

The supervisor assists in developing employees in order to strengthen the organization. He or she gives up the authority to make decisions that are best made by subordinates. This means that the supervisor allows subordinates the freedom to make mistakes and learn from them. He or she does not supervise subordinates' decision-making, but allows them the opportunity to develop their own skills. The supervisor lets subordinates know that he or she is willing to help, but not willing to do their jobs for them. The supervisor is not convinced that the best way for employees to learn is by telling them how to solve a problem. This results in those subordinates becoming dependent on the supervisor. The supervisor allows employees the opportunity to achieve and be credited for it.

An organization's most valuable resource is its people. By empowering employees who perform delegated jobs with the authority to manage those jobs, supervisors free themselves to manage more effectively. Successfully training future supervisors means delegating authority. This gives employees the concrete skills, experience, and the resulting confidence to develop themselves for higher positions. Delegation provides better managers and a higher degree of efficiency. Thus, collective effort, resulting in the organization's growth, is dependent on delegation of authority.

RESPONSIBILITY AND ACCOUNTABILITY

Equally important to authority is the idea that when an employee is given responsibility for a job, he or she must also be given the degree of authority necessary to carry it out. Thus, for effective delegation, the authority granted to an employee must equal the assigned responsibility. Upon accepting the delegated task, the employee has incurred an obligation to perform the assigned work and to properly utilize the granted authority. Responsibility is the obligation to do assigned tasks. The individual employee is responsible for being proficient at his or her job. The supervisor is responsible for what employees do or fail to do, as well as for the resources under their control. Thus, responsibility is an integral part of a supervisor's authority.

Responsibilities fall into two categories: individual and organizational. Employees have individual responsibilities to be proficient in their job. They are responsible for their actions. Nobody gives or delegates individual responsibilities. Employees assume them when they accept a position in the organization. Organizational responsibilities refer to collective organizational accountability and include how well departments perform their work. For example, the supervisor is responsible for all the tasks assigned to his or her department, as directed by the manager.

When someone is responsible for something, he or she is liable, or accountable to a superior, for the outcome. Thus, accountability flows upward in the organization. All are held accountable for their personal, individual conduct. Accountability is answering for the result of one's actions or omissions. It is the reckoning, wherein one answers for his or her actions and accepts the consequences, good or bad. Accountability establishes reasons, motives and importance for actions in the eyes of managers and employees alike. Accountability is the final act in the establishment of one's credibility. It is important to remember that accountability results in rewards for good performance, as well as discipline for poor performance.

DELEGATION PROCESS

The delegation process has five phases: (1) preparing, (2) planning, (3) discussing, (4) auditing, and (5) appreciating. The first step in delegating is to identify what should and should not be delegated. The supervisor should delegate any task that a subordinate performs better. Tasks least critical to the performance of the supervisor's job can be delegated.

Any task that provides valuable experience for subordinates should be delegated. Also, the supervisor can delegate the tasks that he or she dislikes the most. But, the supervisor should not delegate any task that would violate a confidence.

- Preparing includes establishing the objectives of the delegation, specifying the task that needs to be accomplished, and deciding who should accomplish it.
- Planning is meeting with the chosen subordinate to describe the task and to ask the subordinate to devise a plan of action. As Andrew Carnegie once said, "The secret of success is not in doing your own work but in recognizing the right man to do it." Trust between the supervisor and employee-that both will fulfil the commitment-is most important.
- Discussing includes reviewing the objectives of the task as well as the subordinate's plan of action, any potential obstacles, and ways to avoid or deal with these obstacles. The supervisor should clarify and solicit feedback as to the employee's understanding. Clarifications needed for delegation include the desired results (what not how), guidelines, resources available, and consequences (good and bad). Delegation is similar to contracting between the supervisor and employee regarding how and when the work will be completed. The standards and time frames are discussed and agreed upon. The employee should know exactly what is expected and how the task will be evaluated.
- Auditing is monitoring the progress of the delegation and making adjustments in response to unforeseen problems.
- Appreciating is accepting the completed task and acknowledging the subordinate's efforts.

Since motivation influences productivity, supervisors need to understand what motivates employees to reach peak performance. It is not an easy task to increase employee motivation because employees respond in different ways to their jobs and their organization's practices. Motivation is the set of processes that moves a person toward a goal. Thus, motivated behaviors are voluntary choices controlled by the individual employee. The supervisor (motivator) wants to influence the factors that motivate employees to higher levels of productivity.

Factors that affect work motivation include individual differences, job characteristics, and organizational practices. Individual differences are the personal needs, values, and attitudes, interests and abilities that people bring to their jobs. Job characteristics are the aspects of the position that determine its limitations and challenges. Organizational practices are the rules, human resources policies, managerial practices, and rewards systems of an organization. Supervisors must consider how these factors interact to affect employee job performance.

Motivational Theories

The purpose of behavior is to satisfy needs. A need is anything that is required, desired, or useful. A want is a conscious recognition of a need. A need arises when there is a difference in self-concept (the way I see myself) and perception (the way I see the world around me). The presence of an active need is expressed as an inner state of tension from which the individual seeks relief.

Many methods of employee motivation have been developed. The study of work motivation has focused on the motivator (supervisor) as well as the motivatee (employee). Motivation theories are important to supervisors attempting to be effective leaders. Two primary approaches to motivation are content and process.

The content approach to motivation focuses on the assumption that individuals are motivated by the desire to fulfil inner needs. Content theories focus on the needs that motivate people.

Maslow's Hierarchy of Needs identifies five levels of needs, which are best seen as a hierarchy with the most basic need emerging first and the most sophisticated need last. People move up the hierarchy one level at a time. Gratified needs lose their strength and the next level of needs is activated. As basic or lower-level needs are satisfied, higher-level needs become operative. A satisfied need is not a motivator. The most powerful employee need is the one that has not been satisfied. Abraham Maslow first presented the five-tier hierarchy in 1942 to a psychoanalytic society and published it in 1954 in Motivation and Personality (New York: Harper and Row).

Level I: Physiological needs are the most basic human needs. They include food, water, and comfort. The organization helps to satisfy employees' physiological needs by a paycheck.

Level II: Safety needs are the desires for security and stability, to feel safe from harm. The organization helps to satisfy employees' safety needs by benefits.

Level III: Social needs are the desires for affiliation. They include friendship and belonging. The organization helps to satisfy employees' social needs through sports teams, parties, and celebrations. The supervisor can help fulfil social needs by showing direct care and concern for employees.

Level IV: Esteem needs are the desires for self-respect and respect or recognition from others. The organization helps to satisfy employees' esteem needs by matching the skills and abilities of the employee to the job. The supervisor can help fulfil esteem needs by showing workers that their work is appreciated.

Level V: Self-actualization needs are the desires for self-fulfilment and the realization of the individual's full potential. The supervisor can help fulfil self-actualization needs by assigning tasks that challenge employees' minds while drawing on their aptitude and training.

Alderfer's ERG identified three categories of needs. The most important contribution of the ERG model is the addition of the frustration-regression hypothesis, which holds that when individuals are frustrated in meeting higher level needs, the next lower level needs reemerge.

Existence needs are the desires for material and physical well being. These needs are satisfied with food, water, air, shelter, working conditions, pay, and fringe benefits.

Relatedness needs are the desires to establish and maintain interpersonal relationships. These needs are satisfied with relationships with family, friends, supervisors, subordinates, and co-workers.

Growth needs are the desires to be creative, to make useful and productive contributions and to have opportunities for personal development.

McClelland's Learned Needs divides motivation into needs for power, affiliation, and achievement.

Achievement motivated people thrive on pursuing and attaining goals. They like to be able to control the situations in which they are involved. They take moderate risks. They like to get immediate feedback on how they have done. They tend to be preoccupied with a task-orientation towards the job to be done.

Power motivated individuals see almost every situation as an opportunity to seize control or dominate others. They love to influence others. They like to change situations whether or not it is needed. They are willing to assert themselves when a decision needs to be made.

Affiliation motivated people are usually friendly and like to socialize with others. This may distract them from their performance requirements. They will usually respond to an appeal for cooperation.

Herzberg's Two-Factor Theory describes needs in terms of satisfaction and dissatisfaction. Frederick Herzberg examined motivation in the light of job content and contest. (See Work an the Nature of Man, Crowell Publications, 1966.) Motivating employees is a two-step process. First provide hygienes and then motivators. One continuum ranges from no satisfaction to satisfaction. The other continuum ranges from dissatisfaction to no dissatisfaction.

Satisfaction comes from motivators that are intrinsic or job content, such as achievement, recognition, advancement, responsibility, the work itself, and growth possibilities. Herzberg uses the term motivators for job satisfiers since they involve job content and the satisfaction that results from them. Motivators are considered job turn-ons. They are necessary for substantial improvements in work performance and move the employee beyond satisfaction to superior performance. Motivators correspond to Maslow's higher-level needs of esteem and self-actualization.

Dissatisfaction occurs when the following hygiene factors, extrinsic or job context, are not present on the job: pay, status, job security, working conditions, company policy, peer relations, and supervision. Herzberg uses the term hygiene for these factors because they are preventive in nature. They will not produce motivation, but they can prevent motivation from occurring. Hygiene factors can be considered job stay-ons because they encourage an employee to stay on a job. Once these factors are provided, they do not necessarily promote motivation; but their absence can create employee dissatisfaction. Hygiene factors correspond to Maslow's physiological, safety, and social needs in that they are extrinsic, or peripheral, to the job. They are present in the work environment of job context.

Motivation comes from the employee's feelings of accomplishment or job content rather than from the environmental factors or job context. Motivators encourage an employee to strive to do his or her best. Job enrichment can be used to meet higher-level needs. To enrich a job, a supervisor can introduce new or more difficult tasks, assign individuals specialized tasks that enable them to become experts, or grant additional authority to employees.

The process approach emphasizes how and why people choose certain behaviors in order to meet their personal goals. Process theories focus on external influences or behaviors that people choose to meet their needs. External influences are often readily accessible to supervisors.

Vroom's Expectancy Model suggests that people choose among alternative behaviors because they anticipate that particular behaviors will lead to one or more desired outcomes and that other behaviors will lead to undesirable outcomes. Expectancy is the belief that effort will lead to first-order outcomes, any work-related behavior that is the direct result of the effort an employee expends on a job.

Equity is the perception of fairness involved in rewards given. A fair or equitable situation is one in which people with similar inputs experience similar outcomes. Employees will compare their rewards with the rewards received by others for their efforts. If employees perceive that an inequity exists, they are likely to withhold some of their contributions, either consciously or unconsciously, to bring a situation into better balance.

For example, if someone thinks he or she is not getting enough pay (output) for his or her work (input), he or she will try to get that pay increased or reduce the amount of work he or she is doing. On the other hand, when a worker thinks he or she is being paid too much for the work he or she is doing, he or she tends to increase the amount of work. Not only do workers compare their own inputs and outputs; they compare their input/output ratio with the input/output ratio of other workers. If one work team believes they are doing more work than a similar team for the same pay, their sense of fairness will be violated and they will tend to reduce the amount of work they are doing. It is a normal human inclination to want things to be fair.

Bowditch and Buono note (see Bowditch, James L. and Anthony F. Buono, A Primer on Organizational Behavior, 4th, John Wiley & Sons, 1997) that while equity theory was originally concerned with differences in pay, it may be applied to other forms of tangible and intangible rewards in the workplace. That is, if any input is not balanced with some fair output, the motivation process will be difficult. Supervisors must manage the perception of fairness in the mind of each employee. If subordinates think they are not being treated fairly, it is difficult to motivate them.

Reinforcement involves four types of consequence. Positive reinforcement creates a pleasant consequence by using rewards to increase the likelihood that a behavior will be repeated. Negative reinforcement occurs when a person engages in behavior to avoid unpleasant consequences or to escape from existing unpleasant consequences. Punishment is an attempt to discourage a target behavior by the application of negative outcomes whenever it is possible. Extinction is the absence of any reinforcement, either positive or negative, following the occurrence of a target behavior. Employees have questions about their jobs. Can I do what management is asking me to do? If I do the job, will I be rewarded? Will the reward I receive be satisfactory to me?

Reinforcement is based primarily on the work of B.F. Skinner, a psychologist, who experimented with the theories of operant conditioning. Skinner's work shows that many behaviors can be controlled through the use of rewards. In fact, a person might be influenced to change his or her behavior by giving him or her rewards.

Employees who do an exceptionally good job on a particular project should be rewarded for that performance. It will motivate them to try to do an exceptional job on their next project. Employees must associate the reward with the behavior. In other words, the employee must know for what specifically he or she is being rewarded! The reward should come as quickly as possible after the behavior. The reward can be almost anything, but it must be something desired by the employee. Some of the most powerful rewards are symbolic; things that cost very little but mean a lot to the people who get them. Examples of symbolic rewards are things like plaques or certificates.

Values

Each supervisor's approach to management will reflect his or her values, as well as those of the organization. Building trust starts with creating culture based on shared values. Values are traits or qualities having intrinsic worth, such as courage, respect, responsibility, caring, truthfulness, self-discipline, and fairness. Values serve as a baseline for actions and decision-making and guide employees in the organization's intentions and interests. The values driving behavior define the organizational culture. A strong value system or clearly defined culture turns beliefs into standards such as best quality, best performance, most reliable, most durable, safest, fastest, best value for the money, least expensive, most prestigious, best designed or styled, easiest to use. If asked, "What do we believe in?" or "List our organization's values" all employees in the organization should write down the same values. For example, McDonald's values were captured in its motto of "Q.S.C. & V." which stands for quality, service, cleanliness, and value.

Supervisors need to appreciate the significance of values and value systems. Values affect how a supervisor views other people and groups, thus influencing interpersonal relationships. Values affect how a supervisor perceives situations and solves problems. Values affect how a supervisor determines what is and is not ethical behavior. Values affect how a supervisor leads and controls employees. Since employees often base behavior on perceived values it is critical to ensure their perceptions reflect organizational values. Supervisors must communicate, encourage and reinforce the desired values and related behaviors to integrate them into the organizational culture.

Geert Hofstede identified a work-related value framework that has four dimensions: power distance, uncertainty avoidance, individualism, and polarization. Power distance is the attitude to human inequality and relationships to superiors and inferiors in any hierarchy. Uncertainty avoidance is the tolerance for uncertainty that determines choices and rituals to cope with it in social structures and belief systems. Individualism is the relationship between the individual and the collectivity, especially in the way individuals choose to live and work together. Polarization is the extent to which differences such as masculinity or femininity have implications for social organization and the organizations of beliefs. Every person has a different mental program, based on patterns of thinking, feeling, and acting, which are learned throughout a lifetime. The effects of these differences have many practical implications for those who work or are managers in multinational business and for those involved in international negotiations.

Mission

A mission is a broad definition of a business that differentiates it from all other organizations. It is the justification for the organization's existence. The mission statement is the "touchstone" by which all offerings are judged. In addition to the organization's purpose other key elements of the mission statement should include whom it serves, how, and why. The most effective mission statements are easily recalled and provide direction and motivation for the organization.

Since an organization exists to accomplish something in the larger environment, its specific mission or purpose provides employees with a shared sense of opportunity, direction, significance, and achievement. An explicit mission guides employees to work independently and yet collectively toward the realization of the organization's potential. Thus, a good mission statement gets the emotional bonding and commitment needed. It allows the individual employee to say; "I know how I should do my job differently."

For example, many people might think that The Walt Disney Company's mission is to run theme parks. But, Disney's mission is always moving toward an expanded view. Disney provides entertainment. "Disney's overriding objective is to create shareholder value by continuing to be the world's premier entertainment company from a creative, strategic, and financial standpoint."

Also, many people might think that Revlon's mission is to make cosmetics. Yet, Revlon provides glamour, excitement and innovation. Charles Revson, Revlon's founder understood the importance of mission. He said "In the factory, we make cosmetics; in the store, we sell hope."

Vision

Erich Fromm pointed out; "The best way to predict your future is to create it." A vision might be a picture, image, or description of the preferred future. A visionary has the ability to foresee something and sees the need for change first. He or she challenges the status quo and forces honest assessments of where the industry is headed and how the company can best get there. A visionary is ready with solutions before the problems arise.

A study over the period from 1926 to 1990 found visionary companies that set a purpose beyond making money outperformed other companies in the stock market by more than six to one. Managers require more vision than ever because change is coming faster than ever. Leaders have the ability to make their vision real by engaging the minds, as well as the hearts of others.

Microsoft's early vision statement was "A Computer on Every Desk and In Every Home." (At approximately the same time, President John Akers said IBM's goal was to become a $100 billion company by then end of the century.

At that time IBM sales were $50 billion.) Microsoft's vision has evolved [1998 the "Connected PC and the Connected TV"-the idea of integrating the intelligence and interactivity of PCs with the video and sound of TV] to 2002 "to enable people and businesses throughout the world to realize their full potential."

Life consists in what a man is thinking of all day.--Ralph Waldo Emerson

A goal is an end that the organization strives to attain. However, the supervisor cannot "do" a goal. Supervisors break down processes, analyze them, set objectives and then drive hard to achieve them. Doing the same thing and expecting different results doesn't work. The supervisor must write an objective for what he or she is trying to accomplish. Thus, an objective is the object or aim of an action. It implies an explicit direction for the action to take and a specific quality of work to be accomplished within a given period of time. Objectives reflect the desired outcomes for individuals, groups and organizations. They provide direction for decision-making and a criterion against which outcomes are measured. Thus, objectives are the foundation of planning.

MANAGEMENT BY OBJECTIVES (MBO)

An effective planning tool to help the supervisor set objectives is Management by Objectives (MBO). MBO gained recognition in 1954 with the publication of Peter Drucker's book The Practice of Management. MBO is a collaborative process whereby the manager and each subordinate jointly determine objectives for that subordinate. To be successful MBO programs should include commitment and participation in the MBO process at all levels, from top management to the lowest position in the organization.

MBO begins when the supervisor explains the goals for the department in a meeting. The subordinate takes the goals and proposes objectives for his or her particular job.

The supervisor meets with the subordinate to approve and, if necessary, modify the individual objectives. Modification of the individual's objectives is accomplished through negotiation since the supervisor has resources to help the subordinate commit to the achievement of the objective. Thus, a set of verifiable objectives for each individual are jointly determined, prioritized, and formalized. The supervisor and the subordinate meet periodically to review the latter's progress. Communication is the key factor in determining MBO's success or failure. The supervisor gives feedback and may authorize modifications to the objectives or their timetables as circumstances dictate. Finally, the employee's performance is measured against his or her objectives, and he or she is rewarded accordingly.

Steps in MBO Process

Research has demonstrated that when top management is committed and personally involved in implementing MBO programs, they significantly improve performance. This finding is not surprising when one considers that during the MBO process employees determine what they will accomplish. After all, who knows what a person is capable of doing better than the person does him or herself?

Objectives are the driver of planning processes. It is imperative that top managers safeguard the intention of their goals to facilitate middle and lower management's effective translation and implementation of them. Objectives guide managerial activities such as budgeting, the development of action plans, staffing, and the purchasing of equipment. The organization's success ultimately depends on the combined outcomes of its objectives.

Objectives

Most supervisors set objectives, but not with equal skill. Few, who do not correctly write objectives, will reap MBO's full benefits. An objective is simply a statement of what is to done and should be stated in terms of results. A mnemonic aid to write objectives is SMART (Specific, Measurable, Attainable, Result-oriented, Time-limited).

Specific

An objective must be specific with a single key result. If more than one result is to be accomplished, more than one objective should be written. Just knowing what is to be accomplished is a big step toward achieving it.

What is important to you? Once you clarify what you want to achieve, your attention will be focused on the objective that you deliberately set. You will be doing something important to you.

Measurable

An objective must be measurable. Only an objective that affects behavior in a measurable way can be optimally effective. If possible, state the objective as a quantity. Some objectives are more difficult to measure than others are. However, difficulty does not mean that they cannot be measured. Treatment of salespeople might be measured by looking at the absenteeism and turnover rates among the sales force. Also, salespeople could be asked to fill out a behavioral questionnaire anonymously giving their observations of the supervision they receive. Customer service could be measured by such indices as the number of complaints received, by the number of customers lost, and by customer interviews or responses to questionnaires. Development of subordinates could be measured by determining the number of tasks the subordinate has mastered. Cooperation with other functions could be measured by length of delay in providing requested information, or by peer ratings of degree of cooperation.

Avoid statements of objectives in generalities. Infinitives to avoid include to know, to understand, to enjoy, and to believe. Action verbs are observable and better communicate the intent of what is to be attempted. They include to write, to apply, to recite, to revise, to contrast, to install, to select, to assemble, to compare, to investigate, and to develop.

PROGRESS OUTLOOK

Attainable

An objective must be attainable with the resources that are available. It must be realistic. Many objectives are realistic. Yet, the time it takes to achieve them may be unrealistic. For example, it is realistic to want to lose ten pounds. However, it is unrealistic to want to lose ten pounds in one week.

What barriers stand between you and your objective? How will each barrier be overcome and within what time frame?

Result-oriented

The objective should be central to the goals of the organization. The successful completion of the objective should make a difference.

How will this objective help the organization move ahead? Is the objective aligned with the mission of the organization?

Time-limited

The objective should be traceable. Specific objectives enable time priorities to be set and time to be used on objectives that really matter.

Are the time lines you have established realistic? Will other competing demands cause delay? Will you be able to overcome those demands to accomplish the objective you've set in the time frame you've established?

Meaningful Objectives

Although the rules are difficult to establish, the following may be useful when writing an objective.

1. Start with an action or accomplishment verb. (Use the infinitive form of the verb. This means to start the with "to.")
2. Identify a single key result for each objective.
3. Give the date of the estimated completion.
4. Be sure the objective is one you can control.
5. To test for validity of SMART objectives, ask yourself the following questions.
   - S = Exactly what is my objective?
   - M = What would a good job look like?
   - A = Is my objective feasible?
   - R = Is my objective meaningful?
   - T = Is my objective traceable?

The following fill-in-the-blank equation may be useful when writing an objective.

Objective: To (+ action verb + single key result + target date)

PROCESS OF ORGANIZING

PIM implies the establishment of an organization of water users. In cases of management transfer, the establishment process focuses on a level of user organization where no organization presently exists, that is, at a level of the irrigation network previously managed by the government irrigation agency. Typically this entails organizing federations of user groups at the tertiary level under a secondary canal association. The challenge of creating a new organization of users is perhaps the most central feature of the management transfer process. The act of management transfer from the agency to the users depends upon a user organization that is capable of assuming those management responsibilities.

Before any organizing of the users is carried out, there needs to be a package of incentives in place for both the users and the agency staff whose jobs would be affected by the transfer program.

Such incentives are needed both to make the program work, and to maintain credibility with farmers whose long-term support will be required.

If organizing is attempted before an adequate incentive structure is established, the transfer program could well collapse, thus setting the entire program back by several years, as well as causing short-term hardships to those concerned. Thus, if the incentives are not clear and attractive to farmers, the organizing process should be delayed until the incentives are clarified.

First determine:

Initiate Organizing?

The first step is to decide on the type of organizers who will work directly with farmers in helping establish the organization. [We use the term "water user association" (WUA) to refer to this new organization, although the term, "WUA" can also refer to organizations at the tertiary level of the system which have always been outside the management control of the government irrigation agency.]

In the Philippines, a special cadre of social organizers was recruited and trained by the National Irrigation Administration in the late 1970s and early 80s. These organizers were mostly social workers or social scientists selected for their ability to work easily with farmers in village conditions.

They were trained in irrigation management so they could better understand the technical problems of the farmers they were trying to organize.

The work of the Philippines social organizers was effective, yet this approach has not been widely replicated by irrigation agencies in other countries. The investment and bureaucratic difficulties involved in recruiting new temporary staff from a different discipline has led many irrigation agencies to try other approaches. In Mexico's transfer program, the National Water Commission's own staff were used along with staff from a sister agency, the Institute for Water Technology (IMTA). In addition, a few consultants were brought in on a case by case basis.

In India, some state irrigation departments have relied on extensionists from the Agriculture Department under the Command Area Development Program. Also in India, several NGOs have been involved in organizing, at the request of the irrigation departments.

But the organizers of choice, for most irrigation agencies, will be their own field staff. These staff are already within the bureaucratic structure of the agency, so the lines of authority are clear, there is little additional expense involved, and these staff are already familiar with the physical systems and with the local farmers.

The problems with using irrigation agency field staff for organizing work, however, are considerable. These staff are not necessarily interested in organizing farmers, They have not received any prior training in social work (in most cases), and their superiors have also no training (nor interest) in these tasks. These would-be organizers must be re-trained for their organizing tasks, and just as importantly, their job assignments need to be re-defined to reflect their new role. In addition, their superiors need to be trained and re-oreinted so they understand and appreciate the new role to be played by their field staff.

Training

Assuming that agency staff will be used for the organizing, and assuming that their professional training has been in irrigation engineering, they would need to be re-tooled as organizers. First of all they would need a thorough understanding of the rationale for PIM, so that they can present a clear message both to the farmers and to their own colleagues within the irrigation agency. Secondly, they will need training in communication skills (including listening skills) for effective interaction with the users.

Thirdly, they will need training in social analysis, including an understanding of social stratification (by caste, ethnicity, or class), kinship, patron-client relations, labour relations, religious factors, political affiliation, land tenure (tenants, share-croppers, owners), etc.

And fourthly, they would need training in methods for gathering information from farmers (e.g., participatory rural appraisal) and in methods for organizing farmers.

Getting Training

Irrigation management training institutes?

Universities?

Administrative staff colleges?

NGOs?

What capacity building do these organizations need?

Skills training: TOT course on PIM?

Structural change in the organization itself? (IMTI case)

Financing?

New or clarified mandate?

Building support for capacity building may require training and consensus building at political levels, just to provide an enabling environment for the PIM program to get started.

Then,

Organizing Steps

Note: This assumes there are reasonable incentives for farmers to take over system, and for the government irrigation agency to hand over the system; if not, go back and work on the incentives!

- Organize the organizers: Arrange for supervision/ support for the organizers, and clear lines of communication with Departmental staff responsible for the overall project (Ensure that PIM component of program is well integrated with rest of project).
- Meet the farmers and other irrigation stakeholders/ Discuss plans formulated during participatory design phase:
  - * village head
  - * local administrative officials
  - * local political leaders (MLAs/MPs)
  - * leaders of other farmer organizations (producer cooperatives)
- Identify key power relations among farmers; develop strategy for organizing
- Establish provisional boundaries of the system (through consultation with key power brokers among the farmers); conduct inventory of potential members; draw map showing command area and irrigation system.
- Arrange series of meetings between farmers and Departmental field staff to discuss improvements that need to be made prior to handover.
  - * arrange canal walk-through to discuss specifics of design/infrastructure improvements
  - * discuss general terms of WUA contracts
- Arrange farmer visits to other associations to discuss with those farmers (and invite those farmers to visit new association).

- Organizational Assistance:
  * Help prospective WUA leaders arrange farmer meetings to discuss plans
  * Help formulate/revise by-laws
  * Advise on elections/selections
  * Assist with legal registration
  * Arrange management training for WUA leaders
- Arrange meetings between WUA leaders and Department staff to discuss details of WUA contract and terms of transition phase leading to hand-over;
- Advise on staff recruitment(?)
- Assist with formal hand-over
- Visit periodically to monitor WUA's performance

10

SYSTEM OF ORGANIZING

MEANING AND DEFINITION

One of the main problems that each enterprise faces is to organize the efforts of the people working on common goals. Most of the solutions to this problem originate from the time before computers became available for practically any company. However, it's a general practice even now, that the developers follow the old management scheme when the company is being computerized, whereas modern computers offer unique opportunities for implementing new, far more effective approaches to management. We discovered the limitations of existing management schemes while computerizing a small trading company. Our objective was to develop a system able to assist the office workers in all aspects of their routine work. One of our tasks was a conventional one-to support such activities as taking orders, delivering goods, making a phone call, etc. The other one was more ambitious-to register all completed activities and to help plan new activities based on the completed ones.

We realized very soon that our second objective could not be achieved within the functional management scheme adopted in the company. To cope with our task we started to consider the company's activity as a number of processes (such as "processing an order", "closing a deal") without regard to the way these processes were being managed. As a result a new approach to management was developed which we call a process-oriented management. This approach can be described as a project management without project managers, a project manager's functions, e.g., planning, controlling the execution of activities, etc., being distributed among the workers involved in a particular process.

The main point with the process-oriented management is that it permits a company to gain full control over all the processes within the frame of the existing, often functionally-oriented, organizational structure. This type of management facilitates also the communication between the workers involved in the same process, and it provides them with actual information on the state of the process, as well as on all activities performed and planned. Below, we present the main ideas of the process-oriented management, and the requirements for a computer system needed to support it.

We tried our best to do that in a very informal way to make it easily understood by all concerned. It should also be mentioned that the author is not a specialist in the field of management, but he worked with experts on management throughout the project. The paper reflects a fresh view of an application developer not spoiled by the experience of the pre-computer management era.

The rest of this paper is organized as follows. In section 2, we outline our view on the management of routine work. In section 3, we present the main principles of the process-oriented management. We look at existing approaches to management of the routine work-the function-oriented management and project-oriented management, and then move on to describing the ways of transforming the project-oriented management into the process-oriented one. We discuss the process-oriented management without regards to computer systems, however, this type of management can't be implemented without computers.

Requirements for a computer system designed to support the process-oriented management are discussed in section

4. In section 5, we discuss the major issues of the development and implementation of such systems. In section 6, we present a short summary of our practical and research work that lead to the development of a process-oriented approach to management.

ROUTINE WORK MANAGEMENT

It's generally recognized that the main objective of management is to ensure a successful achievement of a company's goals at minimal costs. A company has several different types of goals to achieve at any given moment-long-term, short-term, etc. As we are concerned with the management of routine work, it's the "conventional" everyday goals that are of primary interest to us; we call them "operational" goals. A typical operational goal for a trading company is, for example, to "drive" an incoming order through a delivery to receiving payment within certain time limits. A typical operational goal for a hospital is to administer the appropriate treatment to a patient that would lead to his discharging from the hospital. A typical operational goal for a software development company is to build a software system according to the specifications. But for the section of technical support of such company, a typical operational goal is to process a bug report so that the bug is fixed or/and a work-around solution is found.

Though operational goals may be quite unsophisticated, they, nevertheless, constitute the backbone of any business, as they have to be achieved on a day-to-day basis to ensure the proper functioning of the company. The character of operational goals depends on the type of business, but they have a number of common features:

- operational goals pop up more or less regularly;
- there is, usually, a standard procedure for achieving the operational goals of a given kind, which doesn't mean, of course, that a particular goal can't be approached in a different way if needed;

- there is often a set time limit for achieving an operational goal. If the goal is impossible to achieve within the time limit, it is discarded in a standard way.

To achieve an operational goal, a series of activities should be completed. For example, a series of activities aimed at getting payment for an incoming order includes delivery of goods and sending an invoice to the customer. This series may include more items in certain circumstances, for example, if the ordered goods are out of stock, they should be produced or ordered from the suppliers. The activities aimed at achieving an operational goal are not, usually, executed immediately one after another, e.g., if the ordered goods are out of stock, it takes some time to get them from the suppliers. The execution of these activities is a process that continues over some period of time. The main objective for management of operational goals is to ensure that this process results in achieving the goal.

Different activities concerning the same goal can be completed by different workers from different divisions. Another objective of management is, therefore, to coordinate the work of all workers participating in the process of achieving an operational goal.

Process-Oriented Management

Approaches to management of operational goals may be divided in two types-function-oriented and project-oriented. The function-oriented management (Fn-management) is usually used in the environments where a lot of relatively simple operational goals pop up very frequently.

The Fn-management implies that operational goals are handled in a routine manner by the staff where each member has his own function in achieving operational goals. A manager does not coordinate the execution of activities for each goal, workers just react on the incoming documents, phone calls, etc., by completing activities they are assigned, and forwarding the received or newly composed documents further to their colleagues.

The project-oriented management (Pj-management) is usually used with more sophisticated goals such as construction or software projects. The Pj-management implies that a process for a new goal is planned in detail before the work on it starts, and there is someone (e.g., a project manager) who supervises all the work being done.

Fn-management is most cost-effective, but it works poorly when a process of achieving an operational goal deviates from a standard pattern, as it lacks control over individual processes. Pj-management gives full control over an individual process, but it's inefficient when a lot of coexisting processes are involved. There are working environments where one or the other type of management fits well. But in most environments a combination of these two approaches would be the way to obtain both full control over all processes and efficiency.

Below, we discuss our proposals for integration of the Fn-and Pj-managements. The result is a new type of management which we call the process-oriented management, or Pc-management, for short. This name highlights the main objective of the Pc-management-to control the processes, in contrast to Fn-management that places the emphasis on the execution of activities, and the Pj-management that emphasizes plans.

We describe the Pc-management here in the following way. We consider an environment typical for the function-oriented management-a trading company, and try to introduce the project-oriented management in it. The process-oriented management is presented thus as a result of tailoring the project-oriented approach to fit a different kind of environment. We find this way most convenient for discussing our ideas, but it's not, naturally, the only possible one.

The Pc-management is based on the notions of "orgobject", "history" and "dynamic and distributed planning", which we can now turn our attention to.

Orgobjects

The Pj-management involves developing a detailed plan for achieving a project's goal before the work on the project can start. This plan is premised on certain assumptions that may turn out wrong after the project is under way. The plan should then be adapted to the changed conditions. For this purpose, a clear picture of the current state of the project is required to figure out what should be done to complete the project.

A project often involves developing some product that is a physical object, e.g. a software system, a building, etc. This product comes into existence in some form already at the earlier stages of the project, e.g. a half-ready software system or a building under construction.

This half-ready product serves as a good representation of the current state of the project. As the half-ready product can be studied without regards to how it has been produced, the plan can be revised without going into details of the project's history.

In cases where the Fn-management is involved, there is no half-ready product to represent the current state of achieving an operational goal. A kind of an abstract object that contains all information on the current state of the process would be helpful here. As it would serve as an organizing device for achieving the goal, we call it an "orgobject".

For example, an orgobject representing a process of "Get payment for an incoming order" may be a record that contains information on: the name and address of the buyer, a description of each kind of goods ordered, the quantity and price per unit of each kind, the quantities of goods already delivered; the amount of money invoiced; the amount of money received. Having this orgobject, the conditions for the successful achievement of the "get payment" goal could be formulated as follows:

- have the numbers representing the quantities of 'goods ordered' and 'goods delivered' equal for each goods kind,
- have 'money invoiced' equal to the sum of 'ordered' multiplied by 'price per unit' for all goods kinds, and
- have 'money received' equal to 'money invoiced'.

As the process develops, the corresponding orgobject should change so that it reflects all the time the current state of the process. As soon as some activity is completed, the orgobject representing the process is to be modified. Thus, in the above example, after the delivery (full or partial), the quantities of the goods delivered are modified; if the customer has changed the order, the types and quantities of the goods ordered are modified, etc. To ensure that the orgobjects are always up-to-date, the routines for every type of activity should list not only the operations required for completing the activity (e.g., packing and shipping for delivery), but also instructions for the appropriate modifications of the relevant orgobjects.

Thus, the current state of an orgobject reflects the overall result of all activities completed earlier, and shows what actions should be taken to achieve the goal. To return to our example, if the quantity of the goods ordered is greater than the quantity of the goods delivered, the missing goods are to be delivered. If, on the other hand, the quantity of the goods ordered is less than the quantity of the goods delivered, then the customer should be asked to return some of the goods. Other examples: if the amount of money invoiced exceeds the payment received, then the customer should pay the difference. If the amount of the money received exceeds that of invoiced, then a credit note should be issued.

History

The current state of an orgobject contains only the result of the completed activities, but not a list of them, e.g.: the quantity of the goods delivered, but not the number of separate deliveries; the amount of money invoiced, but not the number of separate invoices, etc.

This is OK if all goes as it should. But if something goes wrong, e.g., some goods sent off did not arrive, then the information on all activities performed is vital when figuring out what actions should be taken. This information can be collected through logging all the activities completed in the frame of the given process.

Let's consider the following logging scheme. Every time a worker executes an activity, he/she doesn't physically change the previous state of the relevant orgobject. He/she makes a new record instead which contain the new state of the orgobject and leaves the former one unchanged. For example, after a delivery, a new record is made containing the same information as the previous one except the information on the quantities of the goods delivered. The latter is updated according to the packing list.

The record on the previous state of an orgobject is placed in a special file containing the history of the given orgobject. The worker who completes an activity composes also a report where he/she records: the kind of activity completed, the name of a person who completed it, the date, time, comments, etc. This report is saved together with the previous state of the orgobject in the history file.

Given two consequent states of an orgobject and an activity report, we can reconstruct exactly what happened during the activity execution. For example, in case of delivery, we know exactly by whom and when the goods were delivered, and in what quantities. Thus, our log provides an easy access to the information on both the activity performed, and the state of events before and after it was performed.

Dynamic and Distributed Planning

As it was mentioned above, the Pj-management involves designing a detailed plan for each new process. If we try to apply the same to a Fn-management environment, two problems would arise:

- as Fn-processes are often trivial, their plans would be trivial too, e.g.: 'delivering goods'-'invoicing the buyer'-'getting payment'. It would be meaningless to record such plan for every process (and there are many in this kind of environments),
- unpredictable external events that often occur in Fn-management environments would demand revising the whole plan, e.g.: a customer has changed his order-additional delivery can be required, an invoice is to be sent later than it was initially planned, etc.

Dynamic planning is our answer to these problems. Dynamic planning involves planning only the first few activities at the first stage. As soon as one or several of these are completed, new activities are planned with regard to the emerging state of the relevant orgobject (and standard routines adopted in the company). For example, after a delivery, another delivery is planned if not all ordered goods have been delivered, or invoicing is planned if all goods have been delivered.

The use of dynamic planning is fully beneficial in case of processes that follow a standard pattern. Otherwise, the usual planning is preferable. In case the character of the process (standard/deviating) is difficult to foresee, dynamic planning can be used at first, followed by conventional planning if necessary.

Another poser when trying to introduce the Pj-management in an Fn-environment is how to supervise a process. In cases where the Pj-management is involved, there is usually a project manager who supervises the execution of planned activities, and corrects the plan if needed.

In an environment typical for the Fn-management, a project manager supervising each process would result in significant overheads. A solution to this can be described as "distributed planning". Distributed planning implies that the worker who has completed a planned activity himself plans the subsequent activities. Moreover, he/she can assign these new activities not only to himself, but to other people too. For example, a worker who completes a delivery himself plans invoicing to be completed by another worker.

Distributed planning doesn't exclude the possibility of a centralized supervision of a process. In fact, a supervisor may intervene at any time and correct the plan if needed. Moreover, any member of staff can consult the supervisor in case he/she has some problems with his/her work on a particular process. He/she can do it by planning a special activity, e.g., "asking for help", and assigning his/her supervisor to complete it.

Let's have a look at the issue of implementing dynamic and distributed planning. Above, we considered orgobjects and plans as separate entities. Now, we put a plan inside the orgobject representing the corresponding process. As a result an orgobject besides the information on the current state of the process (e.g., on the customer, goods, delivery and payment) will also include a list of planned activities (e.g., delivery, invoicing, etc.), each of them containing information on what should be done, who's to do that and when.

Thus, a plan becomes part of an orgobject. Consequently, we can treat correction of the plan as one of the operations of changing the orgobject in the course of completing an activity. In section 3.1, we've already mentioned that instructions for modifying orgobjects should be included in the working procedures for each type of activities. To ensure proper dynamic planning, these instructions should embrace modification of the process's plan. In a simple case, a worker who has completed an activity modifies the relevant orgobject by removing this activity from the list of planned activities. In more complex cases, he/she adds new activities to the list, and/or removes some other activities from it.

Being an integral part of the orgobject representing a process, a plan is subjected to the logging we described above. As a result, all acts of replanning are registered in the same way as other modifications of orgobjects. Thus, for example, the name of a person who modified the plan is recorded, which may prove to be useful in case of conflicts.

Advantages

The main advantage of the Pc-management is its flexibility. The Pc-management permits to choose the optimum approach to coping with each process, and within the same management scheme. Thus, simple processes that follow a standard pattern are dealt with in a completely decentralized manner, whereas some more sophisticated case will be dealt with by centralized individual planning and supervising. Moreover, the same process may be treated differently at different stages. For example, it may be started as a standard one, but later it can be planned and supervised individually. As a result, full control over all kinds of processes is gained and efficiency is not sacrificed.

Another important thing is that the Pc-management is not bound to any particular type of organizational structure. It can be used both in case the same member of staff completes all the activities required for achieving an operational goal, and in case each activity type is assigned to a particular worker. This permits to preserve the same management scheme when the organizational structure is changed, e.g., in case of a company's expansion.

Some other advantages are as follows:

1. Orgobjects provide a perfect insight into the company's state of affairs. The information stored in the orgobjects is of great help to the management staff

as it permit to quickly evaluate the state of a process (without going into its history). It also helps to give prompt answers to customers' questions. This kind of information is not easily obtainable when traditional managements schemes are used. Thus, when the Fn-management is used, only the information on the executed activities of a given type is easily accessible, and when the Pj-management is used, only the information on the state of the plans execution is easily accessible.

2. Histories of orgobjects permit to easily trace all the activities completed on a given process, which helps to devise plans for complicated cases. They are also a very important source of data for all kinds of statistical analysis, and other types of information processing required for decision-making.
3. The company's staff becomes goal-and process-conscious, as it is easy for any person to overview all the activities (one's own and those of others) completed in a process he/she is involved in. The history of old orgobjects is useful for "learning by example", which may help a worker to find solutions in difficult cases. The goal-and process-consciousness isn't easy to acquire with a traditional management scheme. Under the Fn-management, a worker doesn't see how a process he/she's in is accomplished. His/her personal goal becomes to complete as efficient as possible the activities he/she is responsible for. That may result in, e.g., a seller concentrating on making telephone calls most of which don't get him to closing a deal.
4. The Pj-management emphasizes following the schedule, which becomes the main goal of the workers engaged in a project. There is a danger that the workers do not keep their eyes open for changes in the surrounding world, which is, e.g., the main reason why large software projects often produce out-of-day systems.

5. As all the information on the past is being stored, the management staff is in a better position concerning various kinds of conflicts, internal conflicts among workers engaged in the same process, and external ones, e.g., with customers or suppliers.
6. Distributed planning is a very powerful tool for coordinating the work which makes unnecessary the intensive communication (exchanges of documents, phone calls, etc.) among the workers engaged in the same processes. They get the required information from the current states of orgobjects and their histories.

An Orgsystem Wanted

Let's imagine you are fascinated by the Pc-management and decide to implement it in your company. A lot of orgobjects start circulating around, each accompanied by a huge history file. You don't find the one you need, you never know which of the orgobjects contains the planned activities assigned to you, and when these activities should be completed. You strove for a better order and got yourself into a mess. And, as if that were not enough, you have a lot of extra work to do. You should construct a new state of an orgobject for each completed activity, and remember to put the new activities on the list and assign them to yourself and others. You wanted to improve the efficiency, but it sinks instead.

There is no need to worry, there is a means to restore the order and efficiency, and that's, naturally a computer system. It's primary aim is to make you happy with the Pc-management doing away with the chaos, that's why we call it an "organizing system", or orgsystem for short.

Let's have another look at the Pc-management, this time supported by an orgsystem. Orgobjects do not circulate between various members of the staff who are to work with them, they stay in the same place together with their history and plans, and are easily accessible to all workers involved.

All planned activities assigned to a given individual appear immediately in his/her personal calendar, so that each worker knows exactly what activities he/she has to complete and when.

An orgsystem provides the means to increase the efficiency by:

- assisting workers in executing each activity,
- providing an extremely user-friendly interface.

These two features are a key to successful implementation of an orgsystem. Without them people would not be motivated to use the system, consequently the Pc-management wouldn't work. Let's look at these features in more detail.

Level of the Help

All operations needed for executing an activity under the Pc-management belong to one of the two groups:

- external operations-operations that affect the "external world", and
- maintaining operations-operations aimed at maintaining orgobjects.

The character of external operation depends on the type of activity, e.g., packing and shipping for delivery, programming and testing for developing a software module, etc. Maintaining operations are the same for all activities. They include:

- updating the information contained in the relevant orgobject,
- correcting the plan,
- logging the preceding state of the orgobject.

An orgsystem assists a worker to complete both the external operations and the maintaining ones.

1. *External Operations:* Level of help which is possible to offer for completing the external operations depends

on the type of activity. For example, programming and testing of a software module are usually performed inside the computer, and they are already fully computerized. Here, an orgsystem should just integrate the existing tools for software development, e.g. editors, debuggers, etc., so that a proper tool is invoked when a user chooses to execute these operations. Packing and shipping are not that easily computerized, not now anyway. But even there, an orgsystem can be helpful to some extent by, e.g., making up a packing list. It's important to give a hand in completing the external operations for each kind of activities. There's a risk otherwise. If some activity is left without the orgsystem's assistance, a worker who completes it can easily forget to make the appropriate changes in the orgobject concerned. In that case, the completed activity will still remain on the list of planned activities and the orgsystem will keep reminding the worker to complete it. There is also a danger that the same activity will be completed several times.

2. *Updating:* Modification of an orgobject can often be done on the basis of the information collected in the process of executing the external operations. For example, an "order" orgobject contains the information on the quantities of the goods already delivered. This information should be updated after each separate delivery. The new quantities can be easily calculated based on the packing list that was made at the previous step, which permits an orgsystem to update the orgobject without assistance from the users.

3. When correcting a plan, a worker is prompted by the system on the appropriate activities to plan next; in simple cases the plan is corrected by the system itself. This is possible, as an orgsystem possesses two type of knowledge:

- on the working procedures used in the company, which helps to plan new activities, and
- on division of responsibilities between different divisions, sections, and workers, which permits to correctly assign new activities.

4. Logging includes two operations:
   - saving the old state of the orgobject, and
   - making a report on the activity completed.

Saving the old state of an orgobject is done by an orgsystem without any user assistance, but an activity report needs a human participation. Even there, an orgsystem helps by automatically supplying the information on what activity has been executed, by whom and when. The rest of the report, e.g., comments, is of course the responsibility of the worker.

User-interface

Conventional computer systems are designed as a set of functions operating on a common database, the main facility of the user-interface being multilevel menus. This type of the user-interface provides the user with a quick access to a function he/she wants to complete. It reflects the objective of a conventional computer system which is to help workers to cope with single activities like updating information, printing a report, etc. An orgsystem objectives are much wider, which brings about the need for a completely different kind of user-interface.

An orgsystem's user-interface permits end-users to freely choose between the object-oriented and activity-oriented way of working with orgobjects, as well as easily switch from one to the other. The object-oriented approach is applied when a user wants to work with a particular orgobject for a longer time. In this case, he/she may need to look at the object's current state and its history, as well as to plan and execute various activities involving the orgobject. The activity-oriented approach is applied when a user wants to complete the same activity for a number of orgobjects. In this case, the dialogue designed for a given activity is repeated for all relevant orgobjects.

The object-oriented way is particularly useful when one worker is responsible for many activities involving an orgobject. It is also the way that management staff can use when there is a need to evaluate the state of a particular process and to devise a plan for a difficult case. The activity-oriented approach is preferable if a worker is responsible for only one type of activities. It's also the right approach to completing simple activities that do not require much human assistance, e.g., printing an invoice, etc.

Another distinguishing feature of an orgsystem's user-interface is that it maintains personal calendars. A personal calendar is a list of activities assigned to a particular worker. The point is that these activities are included in different orgobjects and the calendar permits a perfect overview of a persons' many tasks. The orgsystem offers a variety of ways to use the calendar. A user can browse through his/her calendar, or some parts of it, e.g., to see all activities planned for a particular day, all activities of a certain type, etc. When browsing, he/she can start the execution of his/her activities (activity-oriented approach), or move to the orgobject where a particular activity belongs and start working with this orgobject in the object-oriented manner.

To maintain its user-friendly character, an orgsystem's user-interface should satisfy a number of general requirements. Most important are the following two:

- easy access to all information required for working with orgobjects. For example, when working with an orgobject representing an order, a user should have access to all information related to the customer who ordered goods: his address, previous contacts with him, etc.;

- consistency. There should be standard procedures for navigating to an orgobject, for getting information (e.g., a company's address), for planning, for starting the execution of activities, etc. These standard procedures should be the same for all types of orgobjects and activities.

Joys and Hardships

There are, naturally, technical problems to solve in the development of an orgsystem. The system requirements discussed in the previous section must be met. However, an orgsystem designer's greatest problem is that he starts the development in an environment initially not based on the Pc-management, which makes both design and implementation of an orgsystem far from trivial tasks.

Orgsystems Design

An orgsystem designer should begin with:

- identifying the company's operational goals,
- figuring out what processes are used to achieve them, and
- designing orgobjects to represent these processes.

His/her next task is to review all the working procedures and tailor them to fit the Pc-management scheme (by adding maintaining operations to each activity). This is often a tough job, as there are seldom some written descriptions of the working procedures, and if they exist, they are far from complete. The only way to cope with the job is to try and get the missing information from the company's workers.

The workers would, naturally, know nothing about orgobjects, but they know their job. The conditions in which an orgsystem designer works are similar to those of a linguist who studies a language that exists only in the spoken form. Linguists have special methods permitting them to get the necessary information from the native speakers without teaching them any linguistic notions. Moreover, it's considered a wrong practice to teach informants linguistics, as it may only spoil them.

An orgsystems designer needs similar methods that would permit him to redesign the company's working procedures without introducing the workers into the world of orgobjects, distributed planning, etc. We believe that rapid prototyping is the right method. As soon as a designer has identified the company's operational goals and processes, and designed the orgobjects to represent them, he/she should make a prototype of the system and let the future users test it.

To be able to use prototyping, an orgsystem designer needs appropriate application development tools. These tools should allow him to quickly produce a sketch of the system that has "look-and-feel" of a real system, but lacks processing routines and database access. It's this sketch that we call the prototype of the system. Working with it, a user can navigate among orgobjects in the same way as he would do that when the orgsystem is ready. He can modify existing orgobjects, create new ones, and see how to start different activities. But he can't save the information or see the results of the completed activities.

After the future users have accepted the prototype, the designer can stepwise add database access and processing routines, which would be also done with the help of the above mentioned application development tools.

Implementation

Implementing an orgsystem means introducing the Pc-management in a non-Pc-management environment. This may be achieved in one of two ways:

- by substituting all the old working procedures in the company at once, or
- by gradual introduction of the new working procedures.

The first approach may suit small companies whose workers often switch from one activity type to another. An orgsystem would help to do these switches very quickly, and it would help the workers, who usually have a lot of different things to do, to preserve the order in their affairs. The staff of a small company would easily understand the advantages of using all facilities provided by an orgsystem: object-and activity-oriented ways of working, personal calendars, easy access to the history, etc.

However, in case of large companies, the second approach may be the best choice. Large companies usually, have a lot of workers who are involved only in one or several activities for each process. These workers may believe that an orgsystem is too complex for their simple tasks. It would be difficult for them to see the advantages of the object-oriented user-interface, and their earlier experience of traditional computer systems can only make the things worse.

Luckily, an orgsystem provides a means for working in the activity-oriented manner, which would put the workers competing simple activities at ease. There would be no problem to teach them to use the orgsystem in the activity-oriented way, because it resembles their old manner of doing things. Later, the workers could be taught the object-oriented way as well, which would give them better possibilities to take the initiative and find solutions for difficult cases. But even if most of the office workers continue to use the activity-oriented approach, there would always be some key people who benefit from the object-oriented approach, e.g., management staff.

SUMMARY

Achievements

The notion of the Pc-management came into being when the author together with several colleagues developed an application for supporting sales and marketing activities of a trading company. The system was called "DealDriver" to highlight that it helps the workers to "drive" the deals to the end which is receiving payment. Deals were thus the first type of orgobjects designed. The work on the project started in spring 1989, and the first version of DealDriver was ready in summer 1990. Since then, Dealdriver has been successfully used at our home office to support one of IbisSoft's business activities-reselling of professional software.

The DealDriver project, gave us some valuable insights into the problems of orgsystems development which are summarized in our internal reports. We developed also an experimental version of application development tools to support orgsystems development. These tools were later used for building both prototypes and functioning systems in a number of other application fields, e.g., hospital administration.

Next two subsections discuss some theoretical and technical aspects of orgsystems development. The reader who is not interested in such issues is invited to look over these.

Related Research Fields

Orgsystems development belongs to an application field called groupware. This is a multidisciplinary field where social scientists and computer scientists work together. Some of the computer science fields related to our work are as follows:

- the behaviour of dynamic objects, where the orgobjects belong, is being formalized by the theory of object-oriented systems;
- methods of storing and accessing structured information, which are vital for orgsystems development, are the subject of the database theory. Particularly related to our work are the theories of semantic databases, object-oriented databases, and temporal databases;

- methods of planning for robots are one of AI's (Artificial intelligence) favourite research problems. The results obtained there may in some cases be directly applied to the management field. For example, the difference between classical and reactive planning corresponds to the difference between the pure Pj-and Fn-management.

Working System

The main ideas of the Pc-management originate from our previous research work on the CHAOS project [11,12] (CHAOS stands for Concurrent Human-Assisted Object Systems). The project's objective was to work out a formal model for describing distributed interactive systems. This model is based on the notions of objects and connectors.

Objects are used to represent the elements of the "real world", (e.g. people, companies, projects, etc.), whereas connectors are the active elements of the system whose task is to make changes in the objects. A connector may be thought of as a little computer connected to one or several objects. As soon as some of these objects change, the connector changes all the other objects to restore the consistency of the system.

Thus defined, the model has a purely reactive nature, i.e. changes in objects are made as a reaction to changes in other objects. But objects in our model can be complex, i.e. they themselves can contain connectors, which means that a reaction can result in adjusting the system configuration to changes in the environment.

The CHAOS model fitted the management field so well that all we had to do was to use another set of terms. Thus, complex objects became orgobjects, connectors became planned activities, and the principle of reactive reconfiguration of the system was called dynamic and distributed planning. Some of the results of applying the CHAOS model to management field were virtually the same as those from the research works based on the theory of planning. However, being more general than the theory of planning, our model provides a better framework for management automation as it covers all aspects of management not only the issues of planning.

The CHAOS model is abstract, but the approach taken in the DealDriver project was very pragmatic. The objective of the project was to create a working system, not to speculate on the management automation issues. This project differs in many ways from similar research projects. Below we list the most important differences:

1. *Computer Environment*: We worked with PC computers under MS DOS in stand-alone and network versions, whereas research projects are often completed on Unix-based workstations. We used text-based terminals, not a graphic-based windowing environment with a mouse, icons, etc. This environment was chosen because it was the one an average company could easily afford.

2. *Development Tools*: Research workers often choose programming languages popular among computer scientists like Lisp, Prolog, Smalltalk, etc. These languages have a sound theoretical basis (e.g., function theory, logic, etc.), but require a lot of programming when they are used for the development of an application. We made a point of getting the maximum available help with programming by employing commercially available application development tools. We chose JAM from JYACC as a front-end tool, and Btrieve from Novell as a record manager. These tools were of great help to us, as we had limited resources for completing the project (in terms of time and manpower).

3. *Design Principles*: Researchers are often far too interested in the technical issues, such as methods of software design and programming, etc. We concentrated on user-interface issues instead. Our

only principle of programming was: a program should work and permit to easily make necessary changes. All programming was done in C-language, and though our system was object-oriented in a very high degree, we didn't use any object-oriented extension to C.

Thus, two factors contributed to the successful completion of the DealDriver project:

- the use of a powerful abstract model, and
- a pragmatic approach to system development, and we strongly believe that both of them are obligatory for the development of a computer system of a totally new kind.

We are also convinced that there is no need to wait 10-20 years, which it usually takes for new research ideas to be implemented in application systems. New ideas can be implemented today and with the means available now.

11

The Budgeting Process

THE POLICY STATEMENT

The capital improvements program includes all capital projects, regardless of size, financed with state and University funds, and all departmentally funded projects exceeding $100,000 (see the Special Situations section for information on projects less than $100,000). The capital improvements program is an ongoing process that includes:

- Assessing capital needs, opportunities and resources
- Ensuring that potential projects conform with academic priorities & investment strategies
- Establishing priorities for project funding.

Provosts, Chancellors and Vice-Presidents submit their capital improvement needs for review by the Capital Improvements Advisory Committee which recommends systemwide priorities to the Senior Officers of the University. The President submits the capital budget to the Regents.

EXCLUSIONS

Purchases of free-standing instructional and research equipment, even those large enough to be categorized as a "capital expense", should be funded through the operating budget, and should not be submitted to the capital budgeting process. None of the funding sources available for allocation through the capital budget are available for free-standing equipment purchases.

Special Situations

Self-funded projects of less than $100,000 do not require individual approval by the Regents, and are, therefore, excluded from the capital budget process. These projects are handled as follows:

1. Projects are initiated by submitting a Form 1395 request to Capital Planning and Project Management with the dean's sign-off that the proposed project:
   * Conforms with academic priorities of the University
   * Has adequate funding identified
2. Projects are briefly reviewed to ensure that the proposed project:
   * Is within a facility worth investment
   * Will not significantly increase the cost of maintaining and operating the facility
   * Addresses code compliance issues
   * Causes no negative impact on adjacent space/ facilities
   * Conforms with campus master planning principles
3. Projects that meet the preceding criteria will be scheduled for implementation immediately. Projects that do not appear to satisfy all of these criteria will be referred to the CIAC for review and recommendation, and to the Senior Officers for concurrence.
4. If during the planning and design stage the cost of a project increases beyond the $100,000 threshold, the project will be considered in the next capital budgeting cycle, or if the need is urgent, it may be handled as an amendment to the capital budget, requiring the review and recommendation of the CIAC, the concurrence of the Senior Officers, and the approval of the Regents.

Purchases of free-standing instructional and research equipment, even those large enough to be categorized as a "capital expense", should be funded through the operating budget, and should not be submitted to the capital budgeting process. None of the funding sources available for allocation through the capital budget are available for free-standing equipment purchases. However, if the equipment purchases require adjustments to building systems (examples: expanded electrical capacity, HVAC modification) or remodelling of space, those facility improvements should be submitted to the capital budgeting process in accordance with the definitions regarding project size and funding source contained in Section C. A department purchasing equipment which requires building adjustments must either invest departmental funds to achieve those modifications, or must request central funds through the capital budgeting process. If the purchase of equipment represents a high programmatic priority, the priorities for distributing capital resources may be influenced.

THE REASON BEHIND

To assist the President in preparing the capital budget and capital improvements program. To facilitate informed investment decisions and promote effective management of existing capital assets.

SUBMITTING A PROJECT

Procedure

Types of Projects

All projects meeting the following definitions must be submitted to the capital budgeting process:

- Projects requesting central or state funding, regardless of size. Central and state funding sources include fire and life safety, ADA improved access, hazardous materials abatement, repair and replacement, program accommodation remodelling, internal loans, central reserves, University bonds and state bonds.

- Self-funded projects which exceed $100,000. Self-funding sources include departmental funds (O&M, ISO, ICR, gifts and grants) and fees collected by self-supported auxiliary services.

Academic units should submit only projects related to their programmatic needs. Projects that relate exclusively to fire and life safety, improved access, hazardous material abatement, or repair and replacement, should be referred to the units, listed below, that are responsible for addressing those needs.

TYPE OF IMPROVEMENT

Fire and Life Safety-University Building Official.

ADA access-Facilities Management TC Campus FM or Plant Services on other campuses.

Hazardous material-Environmental Health and Safety / TC abatement Campus and air quality FM or Plant Services on other campuses.

Repair and replacement-Facilities Management on TC Campus FM or Plant Services on other campuses.

Submit capital projects to the capital budgeting process in the following manner:

- Departments identify a capital need, complete a project identification form, and submit it to the College or Resource Responsibility Center (RRC). Attach a copy of the project identification form.
- Colleges/RRCs review the requested capital improvement, assign a priority ranking to the request, and submit it to the Provost/Chancellor/Vice President.
- Provosts/Chancellors/Vice Presidents review the requested capital improvement, assign a preliminary

priority ranking to the request, submit it to the Office of Budget and Finance, and present it to the Capital Improvements Advisory Committee (CIAC) budget hearings.

Project Identification

A project identification form must be submitted for all projects proposed for the period, including projects which were previously submitted and incorporated into the Capital Improvements Program. Each annual capital budget and capital improvements program is treated as a new undertaking, and confirmation of each project and its priority ranking is required if it is to remain in the capital improvements program. Project identification forms for projects included in the current capital improvements program are being returned to the Provosts, Chancellors, and Vice Presidents with instructions. Persons proposing those projects may obtain the forms from their Provost, Chancellor, or Vice President in order to improve the project information. If there are no changes, simply resubmit the sheets.

Project Identification Forms must be submitted by Oct. 31

1996 CAPITAL BUDGET

To be considered for inclusion in the Capital Budget, the following conditions must be satisfied:

- Proposed construction projects must have a comprehensive cost estimate prepared by or under the direction of Capital Planning and Project Management. Proposed land or facility acquisitions must have an appraisal approved by the Real Estate Office.
- Proposed projects must have funding available, or have funding contingent upon a pending grant application or private gifts from an active fund raising campaign.

Unless both of these conditions are satisfied, the project will not be included in the Capital Budget, but will instead be placed in a future fiscal year of the capital improvements program.

Prior to Regents' approval of the capital budget, the Office of Budget and Finance will verify the availability of funding for projects which are dependent upon State and University funds. Departments and auxiliaries will be asked to verify the availability of funding for projects to be financed with departmental funds or with fees collected by self-supported auxiliaries by providing a CUFS account number, or by identifying a Foundation account, a grant application, or a fund raising effort.

Verification of funding must be received annually by April 1.

Projects must be identified during the annual budgeting process if they are to be considered for inclusion in the Capital Budget. Projects which are not identified at this time will be deferred to next year's budgeting cycle. Only in extraordinary circumstances will projects be considered as amendments to the approved capital budget during the course of the year. Budget amendments require special review and recommendation by the CIAC, concurrence by the Senior Officers, and approval by the Board of Regents. Implementation of a project cannot proceed until it has been included in the capital budget.

Equipment Purchases

Purchases of free-standing instructional and research equipment, even those large enough to be categorized as a "capital expense", should be funded through the operating budget, and should not be submitted to the capital budgeting process. None of the funding sources available for allocation through the capital budget are available for free-standing equipment purchases.

However, if the equipment purchases being considered will require adjustments to building systems (examples: expanded electrical capacity, HVAC modification) or remodelling of space, those facility improvements should be submitted to the capital budgeting process in accordance with the definitions regarding project size and funding source described at the beginning of this procedure. A department purchasing equipment which requires building adjustments must either invest departmental funds to achieve those modifications, or must request central funds through the capital budgeting process. If the purchase of equipment represents a high programmatic priority, the priorities for distributing capital resources may be influenced.

Discussion Issues and Derivations

Working Capital, Net Working Capital and Non-Cash Working Capital

Working capital is sometimes used to refer only to current assets, while net working capital is defined to be the difference between current assets and current liabilities. Non-cash working capital looks at the difference between non-cash current assets and current liabilities.

In investment analysis, increases in working capital are viewed as cash outflows, because cash tied up in working capital cannot be used elsewhere in the business and does not earn returns. It is the "does not earn returns" component of this definition that would lead us to look at non cash working capital. Firms with significant cash balances today, especially in the US, earn market returns on their cash (by investing in at least T.Bills). Thus, the cash is productive and changes in the cash should not affect our cash flows.

To the degree that cash cannot be invested to earn market returns, and is needed for day-to-day operations, it is appropriate to look at changes in net working capital, with cash included.

Operating versus Capital Expenditures

Accountants draw a distinction between expenditures that yield benefits only in the immediate period or periods (such as labour and material for a manufacturing firm) and those that yield benefits over multiple periods (such as land, buildings and long-lived plant).

The former are called operating expenses and are subtracted from revenues in computing the accounting income, while the latter are capital expenditures and are not subtracted from revenues in the period that they are made. Instead, the expenditure is spread over multiple periods and deducted as an expense in each period-these expenses are called depreciation (if the asset is a tangible asset like a building) or amortization (if the asset is an intangible asset like a patent or a trade mark).

While the capital expenditures made at the beginning of a project are often the largest and most prominent, many projects require capital expenditures during their lifetime. These capital expenditures will reduce the cash available in each of these periods.

Depreciation, Amortization and Other Non-cash Charges

The distinction that accountants draw between operating and capital expenses leads to a number of accounting expenses, such as depreciation and amortization, which are not cash expenses. These non-cash expenses, while depressing accounting income, do not reduce cash flows. In fact, they can have a significant positive impact on cash flows, if they affect the tax liability of the firm. Some non-cash charges reduce the taxable income and the taxes paid by a business. The most important of such charges is depreciation, which, while reducing taxable and net income, does not cause a cash outflow. Consequently, depreciation is added back to net income to arrive at the cash flows on a project.

For projects that generate large depreciation charges, a significant portion of the cash flows can be attributed to the tax benefits of depreciation, which can be written as follows

Tax Benefit of Depreciation = Depreciation * Marginal Tax Rate

While depreciation is similar to other tax deductible expenses in terms of the tax benefit it generates, its impact is more positive because it does not generate a concurrent cash outflow.

Amortization is also a non-cash charge, but the tax effects of amortization can vary depending upon the nature of the amortization. Some amortization, such as the amortization of the price paid for a patent or a trade mark, are tax deductible and reduce both accounting income and taxes. Thus, they provide tax benefits similar to depreciation. Other amortization, such as the amortization of the premium paid on an acquisition (called goodwill), reduces accounting income but not taxable income. This amortization does not provide a tax benefit.

Capital Expenditures and Depreciation

In project analysis, it is important that assumptions about capital expenditures, depreciation and working capital be consistent. For instance,

- If the project is assumed to have a very long life or an infinite life, the firm will have to make much larger capital maintenance expenditure. As a simple rule of thumb, when projects have infinite life, the capital maintenance expenditures should approach depreciation. This will, if nothing else, ensure that the book value of the investment does not decline. More importantly, it is necessary to preserve the earning power of the assets
- For projects with shorter lives, it is possible that capital expenditures occur up front, and that

depreciation in subsequent years is much greater than capital expenditure. The book value of the investment will decline over time to the salvage value.

ROC, Cost of Capital, NPV and EVA

Economic value added is a value enhancement concept that has caught the attention of both firms interested in increasing their value and portfolio managers, looking for good investments. EVA is a measure of dollar surplus value created by a firm or project and is measured by doing the following:

Economic Value Added (EVA) = (Return on Capital-Cost of Capital) (Capital Invested)

where the return on capital is measured using "adjusted" operating income, where the adjustments eliminate items that are unrelated to existing investments, and the capital investment is based upon the book value of capital, but is designed to measure the capital invested in existing assets. Firms which have positive EVA are firms which are creating surplus value, and firms with negative EVA are destroying value.

In the context of investment analysis, the present value of the EVA created by a project should be equal to the net present value of the project.

ROE, Cost of Equity and Equity EVA

While EVA is usually calculated using total capital, it can be easily modified to be an equity measure:

Equity EVA = (Return on Equity-Cost of Equity) (Equity Invested in Project or Firm)

Again, a firm which earns a positive equity EVA is creating value for its stockholders while a firm with a negative equity EVA is destroying value for its stockholders.

Equity EVA may be the better way of thinking about value created for firms where capital is tough to measure (such as banks and insurance companies).

Equity Analysis versus Firm Analysis

An investment project can be analyzed in terms of all of the capital invested in the project (firm) or just from the perspective of the equity investors in the firm. If done consistently, cash flows to the firm discounted at the cost of capital or cash flows to equity discounted at the cost of equity, the two approaches should yield similar results if the following conditions hold:

a. The project is financed using the same mix of debt and equity as is used in the computation of the cost of capital.

b. The debt is assumed to have an interest rate equal to the pre-tax cost of debt

Currency Effects on Investment Analysis

One of the debates that analysts often engage in when doing investment analysis is whether the analysis should be done in one currency or another. Intuitively, an analysis of whether a project is a good or bad one should not depend upon what currency the analysis is done in. The important fact to keep in mind is that cash flows and the discount rate have to be estimated consistently. To convert the analysis from one currency to another would have required the following steps:

Step 1: Estimate the expected exchange rate for each period of the analysis.

While forward rates might be available for some currencies for a few periods, there are very few cases where forward rates will be available for the entire project life. To estimate the expected exchange rate, draw on the purchasing power parity theorem that argues that changes in exchange rates between two countries will reflect differences in inflation in those countries.

Step 2: Convert the expected cashflows from one currency to the other in future periods, using these exchange rates.

Step 3: Discount the expected cashflows at a discount rate, based upon the same currency.

Real versus Nominal Investment Analysis

Investment analyses can be done in terms of real or nominal cash flows. The discount rates have to be defined consistently-real for real cash flows and nominal for nominal cash flows. If done consistently, each analysis should yield the same net present value.

The choice between nominal and real cash flows therefore boils down to one of convenience. When inflation rates are low, it is better to do the analysis in nominal terms since taxes are based upon nominal income. When inflation rates are high and volatile, it is easier to do the analysis in real terms.

Given a choice, I would rather do the analysis in nominal terms, since taxes and financial statements are usually based upon nominal results.

Net Present Value, IRR or Modified IRR

For firms with no capital rationing constraints, net present value is clearly the choice that will maximize firm value the most. For firms with significant capital rationing constraints that will continue into the future, the IRR is likely to be the best solution. For firms with significant capital rationing constraints that will ease over time, the modified IRR is the best solution.

Corporate Strategy and Project Quality

In the process of analyzing new investments in the preceding chapters, we have contended that good projects have a positive net present value and earn an internal rate of return greater than the hurdle rate. While these criteria are certainly valid from a measurement standpoint, they do not address the deeper questions about good projects including the economic conditions that make for a "good" project and why it is that some firms have a more ready supply of "good" projects than others.

Implicit in the definition of a good project--one that earns a return that is greater than that earned on investments of equivalent risk--is the existence of super-normal returns to the business considering the project. In a competitive market for real investments, the existence of these excess returns should act as a magnet, attracting competitors to take on similar investments. In the process, the excess returns should dissipate over time; how quickly they dissipate will depend on the ease with which competition can enter the market and provide close substitutes and on the magnitude of any differential advantages that the business with the good projects might possess. Take an extreme scenario, whereby the business with the good projects has no differential advantage in cost or product quality over its competitors, and new competitors can enter the market easily and at low cost to provide substitutes. In this case the super-normal returns on these projects should disappear very quickly.

An integral basis for the existence of a "good" project is the creation and maintenance of barriers to new or existing competitors taking on equivalent or similar projects. These barriers can take different forms, including

a. *Economies of Scale*: Some projects might earn high returns only if they are done on a "large" scale, thus restricting competition from smaller companies. In such cases, large companies in this line of business may be able to continue to earn super-normal returns on their projects because smaller competitors will not be able to replicate them.

b. *Cost Advantages*: A business might work at establishing a cost advantage over its competitors, either by being more efficient or by taking advantage of arrangements that its competitors cannot use. For example, in the late 1980s, Southwest Airlines was able to establish a cost advantage over its larger competitors, such as American and United Airlines by using non-union employees, the company exploited this cost advantage to earn much higher returns.

c. *Capital Requirements*: Entry into some businesses might require such large investments that it discourages competitors from entering, even though projects in those businesses may earn above-market returns. For example, assume that Boeing is faced with a large number of high-return projects in the aerospace business. While this scenario would normally attract competitors, the huge initial investment needed to enter this business would enable Boeing to continue to earn these high returns.

d. *Product Differentiation*: Some businesses continue to earn excess returns by differentiating their products from those of their competitors, leading to either higher profit margins or higher sales. This differentiation can be created in a number of ways-through effective advertising and promotion (Coca Cola), technical expertise (Sony), better service (Nordstrom) and responsiveness to customer needs.

e. *Access to Distribution Channels*: Those firms that have much better access to the distribution channels for their products than their competitors are better able to earn excess returns. In some cases, the restricted access to outsiders is due to tradition or loyalty to existing competitors. In other cases, the firm may actually own the distribution channel, and competitors may not be able to develop their own distribution channels because the costs are prohibitive.

f. *Legal and Government Barriers*: In some cases, a firm may be able to exploit investment opportunities without worrying about competition because of restrictions on competitors from product patents the firm may own to government restrictions on competitive entry. These arise, for instance, when companies are allowed to patent products or services, and gain the exclusive right to provide them over the patent life.

MANAGEMENT AND PROJECT

In the preceding section we examined some of the factors that determine the attractiveness of the projects a firm will face. While some factors, such as government restrictions on entry, may largely be out of the control of incumbent management, there are other factors that can clearly be influenced by management may largely be out of the control of incumbent management, there are other factors that can clearly be influenced by management.

Considering each of the factors discussed above, for instance, we would argue that a good management team can increase both the number of and the returns on available projects by

- taking projects that exploit any economies of scale that the firm may possess; in addition, management can look for ways it can create economies of scale in the firm's existing operations.
- establishing and nurturing cost advantages over its competitors; some cost advantages may arise from labour negotiations, while others may result from long-term strategic decisions made by the firm. For instance, by owning and developing SABRE, the airline reservation system, American Airlines has been able to gain a cost advantage over its competitors.
- taking actions that increase the initial cost for new entrants into the business; one of the primary reasons Microsoft's was able to dominate the computer software market in the early 1990s was its ability to increase the investment needed to develop and market software programs.

- increasing brand name recognition and value through advertising and by delivering superior products to customers; a good example is the success that Snapple experienced in the early 1990s in promoting and selling its iced tea beverages.
- nurturing markets in which the company's differential advantage is greatest, in terms of either cost of delivery or brand name value. In some cases, this will involve expanding into foreign markets, as both Levi Strauss and McDonalds did in the 1980s in order to exploit their higher brand name recognition in those markets. In other cases, this may require concentrating on segments of an existing market as The Gap did, when it opened its Banana Republic division, which sells upscale outdoor clothing.
- improving the firm's reputation for customer service and product delivery; this will enable the firm to increase both profits and returns. One of the primary factors behind Chrysler's financial recovery in the 1980s was the company's ability to establish a reputation for producing quality cars and minivans.
- developing distribution channels that are unique and cannot be easily accessed by competitors. Avon, for instance, employed large sales foice to go door-to-door to reach consumers who could not be reached by other distribution channels.
- getting patents on products or technologies that keep out the competition and earn high returns; doing so may require large investments in research and development over time. It can be argued that Intel's success in the market for semiconductors can be traced to the strength of its research and development efforts and the patents it consequently obtained on advanced chips, such as the Pentium.

While the quality of management is typically related to the quality of projects a firm possesses, a good management team does not guarantee the existence of good projects.

In fact, there is a rather large element of chance involved in the process; even the best laid plans of the management team to create project opportunities may come to naught if circumstances conspire against them-a recession may upend a retailer, or an oil price shock may cause an airline to lose money.

WORKING CAPITAL MANAGEMENT

Definition

The term working capital refers to the amount of capital which is readily available to an organisation. That is, working capital is the difference between resources in cash or readily convertible into cash (Current Assets) and organisational commitments for which cash will soon be required (Current Liabilities).

Current Assets are resources which are in cash or will soon be converted into cash in "the ordinary course of business".

Current Liabilities are commitments which will soon require cash settlement in "the ordinary course of business".

Thus:

WORKING CAPITAL =
CURRENT ASSETS-CURRENT LIABILITIES

In a department's Statement of Financial Position, these components of working capital are reported under the following headings:

Current Assets

- Liquid Assets (cash and bank deposits)
- Inventory
- Debtors and Receivables

Current Liabilities

- Bank Overdraft
- Creditors and Payables
- Other Short Term Liabilities

Importance

Working capital constitutes part of the Crown's investment in a department. Associated with this is an opportunity cost to the Crown. (Money invested in one area may "cost" opportunities for investment in other areas.) If a department is operating with more working capital than is necessary, this over-investment represents an unnecessary cost to the Crown.

From a department's point of view, excess working capital means operating inefficiencies. In addition, unnecessary working capital increases the amount of the capital charge which departments are required to meet from 1 July 1991.

Various Approaches

The objective of working capital management is to maintain the optimum balance of each of the working capital components. This includes making sure that funds are held as cash in bank deposits for as long as and in the largest amounts possible, thereby maximising the interest earned.

However, such cash may more appropriately be "invested" in other assets or in reducing other liabilities.

Working capital management takes place on two levels:

- Ratio analysis can be used to monitor overall trends in working capital and to identify areas requiring closer management.
- The individual components of working capital can be effectively managed by using various techniques and strategies.

When considering these techniques and strategies, departments need to recognise that each department has a unique mix of working capital components. The emphasis that needs to be placed on each component varies according to department. For example, some departments have significant inventory levels; others have little if any inventory.

Furthermore, working capital management is not an end in itself. It is an integral part of the department's overall management. The needs of efficient working capital management must be considered in relation to other aspects of the department's financial and non-financial performance.

12

Ratio Analysis of the Finance

MEANING

Financial ratio analysis calculates and compares various ratios of amounts and balances taken from the financial statements.

The main purposes of working capital ratio analysis are:

- to indicate working capital management performance; and
- to assist in identifying areas requiring closer management.

Three key points need to be taken into account when analyzing financial ratios:

- The results are based on highly summarised information. Consequently, situations which require control might not be apparent, or situations which do not warrant significant effort might be unnecessarily highlighted;
- Different departments face very different situations. Comparisons between them, or with global "ideal" ratio values, can be misleading;
- Ratio analysis is somewhat one-sided; favourable results mean little, whereas unfavourable results are usually significant.

However, financial ratio analysis is valuable because it raises questions and indicates directions for more detailed investigation.

The following ratios are of interest to those managing working capital:

- working capital ratio;
- liquid interval measure;
- stock turnover;
- debtors ratio;
- creditors ratio.

RATIO OF WORKING CAPITAL

Current Assets divided by Current Liabilities

The working capital ratio (or current ratio) attempts to measure the level of liquidity, that is, the level of safety provided by the excess of current assets over current liabilities.

The "quick ratio" a derivative, excludes inventories from the current assets, considering only those assets most swiftly realisable. There are also other possible refinements.

There is no particular benchmark value or range that can be recommended as suitable for all government departments. However, if a department tracks its own working capital ratio over a period of time, the trends-the way in which the liquidity is changing-will become apparent.

THE LIQUID INTERVAL MEASURE

Liquid Assets divided by Average Operating Expenses

This is another measure of liquidity. It looks at the number of days that liquid assets (for example, inventory) could service daily operating expenses (including salaries).

Stock Turnover

Cost of Sales divided by Average Stock Level

This ratio applies only to finished goods. It indicates the speed with which inventory is sold-or, to look at it from the other angle, how long inventory items remain on the shelves. It can be used for the inventory balance as a whole, for classes of inventory, or for individual inventory items.

The figure produced by the stock turnover ratio is not important in itself, but the trend over time is a good indicator of the validity of changes in inventory policies.

In general, a higher turnover ratio indicates that a lower level of investment is required to serve the department.

Most departments do not hold significant inventories of finished goods, so this ratio will have only limited relevance.

Debtor Ratio

There is a close relationship between debtors and credit sales to third parties (that is, sales other than to the Crown). If sales increase, debtors will increase, and conversely, if sales decrease debtors will decrease.

The best way to explain this relationship is to express it as the number of days that credit sales are carried on the books:

Credit Sales per Period × Days per Period

Average Debtors: Where trading terms are 30 days net cash, and customers buy from day-to-day during the 30 day period and pay 30 days after a statement is rendered, a collection period of 45 days (the average between 30 and 60 days) would be satisfactory.

If the average collection period extends beyond 60 days, debtors are holding cash that should have flowed into the department. This means that the department is unable to satisfy pressing liabilities or to invest that cash. The debtor ratio does not solve the collection problem, but it acts as an indicator that an adverse trend is developing. Remedial action can then be instigated.

Creditor Ratio

This ratio is much the same as the debtor ratio. It expresses the relationship between credit purchases and the liability to creditors. It can be stated as the number of days that credit purchases are carried on the books.

Credit Purchases per Period × Days per Period

Average Creditors: Note that non-credit purchases (such as salaries) and non-cash expenses (such as depreciation) need to be excluded from "credit purchases" and any provisions need to be excluded from "creditors". There is no need to pay creditors before payment is due. The department's objective should be to make effective use of this source of free credit, while maintaining a good relationship with creditors.

As with debtors, if a department has been granted credit terms of 30 days net cash, credit purchases should not be carried on the books for more than an average of 45 days. If payment is withheld for 60 days or more it is likely that creditors will become impatient and impose stricter and less convenient trading terms-for example, "cash on delivery". The Public Finance Act 1989 (section 49) places a legal constraint on the amount of credit allowed to a department. It restricts to a maximum of 90 days the purchase of goods and services through the use of a credit card or suppliers' credit.

PARTICULAR STRATEGIES

Inventories

Inventories are lists of stocks-raw materials, work in progress or finished goods-waiting to be consumed in production or to be sold. The total balance of inventory is the sum of the value of each individual stock line. Stock records are needed:

- to provide an account of activity within each stock line;
- as evidence to support the balances used in financial reports.

A department also needs a system of internal controls to efficiently manage stocks and to ensure that stock records provide reliable information.

Departmental financial reports show only the total inventory balance. Analysts from outside the department can examine this balance by using ratio analysis or other techniques. However, this gives only a limited assessment of inventory management and is not adequate for internal management. Good financial management necessitates the careful analysis of individual inventory lines.

Inventory management is an important aspect of working capital management because inventories themselves do not earn any revenue. Holding either too little or too much inventory incurs costs.

Costs of carrying too much inventory are:

- opportunity cost of foregone interest;
- warehousing costs;
- damage and pilferage;
- obsolescence;
- insurance.

Costs of carrying too little inventory are:

- stockout costs:
    * lost sales;
    * delayed service.

- ordering costs:
  - * freight;
  - * order administration;
  - * loss of quantity discounts.

Carrying costs can be minimised by making frequent small orders but this increases ordering costs and the risk of stock-outs. Risk of stock-outs can be reduced by carrying "safety stocks" (at a cost) and re-ordering ahead of time.

The best ordering strategy requires balancing the various cost factors to ensure the department incurs minimum inventory costs. The optimum inventory position is known as the Economic Reorder Quantity (ERQ).

There are a number of mathematical models (of varying complexity) for calculating ERQ. (Any standard accounting text will provide examples of these).

Analytical review of inventories can help to identify areas where inventory management can be improved. Slow moving items, continual stockouts, obsolescence, stock reconciliation problems and excess spoilage are signals that stock lines need closer analysis and control.

However, it is important to keep an overall perspective. It is not cost-effective to closely manage a large number of low value inventory lines, nor is it necessary. A usual feature of inventories is that a small number of high value lines account for a large proportion of inventory value.

The "80/20" rule (PARETO) predicts that 80% of the total value of inventory is represented by only 20% of the number of inventory items. Those high value lines need reasonably close management. The remaining 80% of inventory lines can be managed using "broad-brush" strategies.

The overall management philosophy of an organisation can affect the way in which inventory is managed. For example, "Just In Time" (JIT) production management organises production so that finished goods are not produced until the customer needs them (minimising finished goods carrying costs), and raw materials are not accepted from suppliers until they are needed. (Large organisations have the power to insist that suppliers hold stocks of raw materials and thereby pass the carrying cost back to the supplier).

Thus, JIT inventory strategies reduce bottlenecks and stock holding costs.

In summary:

- There is a trade-off to be made between carrying costs, ordering costs, and stockout costs. This is represented in the Economic Reorder Quantity (ERQ) model.
- Inventories should be managed on a line-by-line basis using the 80/20 rule.
- Analytical review can help to focus attention on critical areas.
- Inventory management is part of the overall management strategy.

Debtors

Debtors (Accounts Receivable) are customers who have not yet made payment for goods or services which the department has provided.

The objective of debtor management is to minimise the time-lapse between completion of sales and receipt of payment. The costs of having debtors are:

- opportunity costs (cash is not available for other purposes);
- bad debts.

Debtor management includes both pre-sale and debt collection strategies.

Pre-sale strategies include:

- offering cash discounts for early payment and/or imposing penalties for late payment;
- agreeing payment terms in advance;
- requiring cash before delivery;
- setting credit limits;
- setting criteria for obtaining credit;
- billing as early as possible;
- requiring deposits and/or progress payments.

Post-sale strategies include:

- Placing the responsibility for collecting the debt upon the center that made the sale;
- Identifying long overdue balances and doubtful debts by regular analytical reviews;
- Having an established procedure for late collections, such as
    * a reminder;
    * a letter;
    * cancellation of further credit;
    * telephone calls;
    * use of a collection agency;
    * legal action

Creditors

Creditors (Accounts Payable) are suppliers whose invoices for goods or services have been processed but who have not yet been paid.

Organisations often regard the amount owing to creditors as a source of free credit. However, creditor administration systems are expensive and time-consuming to run. The overriding concern in this area should be to minimise costs with simple procedures. While it is unnecessary to pay accounts before they fall due, it is usually not worthwhile to delay all payments until the latest possible date., Regular weekly or fortnightly payment of all due accounts is the simplest technique for creditor management.

Electronic payments (direct credits) are cheaper than cheque payments, considering that transaction fees and overheads more than balance the advantage of delayed presentation. Some suppliers are reluctant to receive payments by this method, but in view of the substantial cost advantage (and the advantages to the suppliers themselves) departments may wish to encourage suppliers to accept this option. However, electronic payments are likely to be used in conjunction with, rather than as a replacement for, cheque payments.

THE CASH AND BANK

Good cash management can have a major impact on overall working capital management.

The key elements of cash management are:

- cash forecasting;
- balance management;
- administration;
- internal control.

Cash Forecasting: Good cash management requires regular forecasts. In order for these to be materially accurate, they must be based on information provided by those managers responsible for the amounts and timing of expenditure. Capital expenditure and operating expenditure must be taken into account. It is also necessary to collect information about impending cash transactions from other financial systems, such as creditors and payroll.

Balance Management: Those responsible for balance management must make decisions about how much cash should at any time be on call in the Departmental Bank Account and how much should be on term deposit at the various terms available.

There are various types of mathematical model that can be used. One type is analogous to the ERQ inventory model. Linear programming models have been developed for cash management, subject to certain constraints. There are also more sophisticated techniques.

Administration: Cash receipts should be processed and banked as quickly as possible because:

- They cannot earn interest or reduce overdraft until they are banked;
- Information about the existence and amounts of cash receipts is usually not available until they are processed.

Where possible, cash floats (mainly petty cash and advances) should be avoided. If, on review, the only reason that can be put forward for their existence is that "we've always had them", they should be discontinued. There may be situations where they are useful, however. For example, it may be desirable for peripheral parts of departments to meet urgent local needs from cash floats rather than local bank accounts.

Internal Control: Cash and cash management is part of a department's overall internal control system. The main internal cash control is invariably the bank reconciliation. This provides assurance that the cash balances recorded in the accounting systems are consistent with the actual bank balances. It requires regular clearing of reconciling items.

Other Factors

Working capital, defined as the difference between current assets and current liabilities, may also include the following factors:

- prepayments to creditors;
- current portions of long-term liabilities;
- revenue received before it has been earned;
- provisions.

However, decisions on working capital management usually exclude these factors, so they have not been included in this booklet.

CONCLUSION

Good management of working capital is part of good financial management. Effective use of working capital will contribute to the operational efficiency of a department; optimum use will help to generate maximum returns.

Ratio analysis can be used to identify working capital areas which require closer management. Various techniques and strategies are available for managing specific working capital items.

Debtors, creditors, cash and in some cases inventories are the areas most likely to be relevant to departments.

13

HOTEL INDUSTRY: PRESENT STATUS

The hospitality industry is growing at a faster rate than ever envisaged and today it has no boundaries. So high is the confidence in this industry that the only restriction is ambition. Over 250 million people around the world are estimated to be employed in this sector alone and the statistics indicate that one job is created in every two and a half seconds by the hospitality industry. Being a trade that encompasses industries like aviation, shipping, entertainment, catering, multiplexes, shopping malls, call centers and of course hotels and restaurants, the opportunities are pouring in with exciting career, assured job, handsome pay packets and above all international recognition and job satisfaction.

NEED OF HOTEL MANAGEMENT

For a professional this is a very lucrative segment capable of offering a long growth oriented career. The hotel sector itself requires a large amount of well trained manpower with excellent skill in housekeeping, food & beverage service and production, marketing, accounting, security, engineering, fire fighting, public relations and so on. A hospitality professional can find job opportunity in customer relations, sales and marketing and event management.

In this fast changing world, the hospitality industry has become the ideal place for those having an inborn talent to mingle with people, work with them and serve them. The young entrants have to come up with an open mind to explore the challenging world of hospitality business. They shall need to be multi skilled, talented and proactive not only to stay afloat but also to stay in demand in the challenging times that lie ahead.

THE ROYAL GROUP

Division of Hotel

The entry of Royal Group into the hospitality industry was by opening an ethnic village resort namely Royal Village in close harmony with the nature in the suburbs of Cochin. The century old traditional Farm House which stands as a testimony of ancient Kerala lifestyle attracting domestic and international tourists alike symbolizes the desire of the group to preserve and protect the culture and heritage of our country. Munnar is best known for its personalized and intimate services offered. This luxury hotel with its exceptional five star facilities may be perhaps the only one of its kind in the state with state of the art Discotheque, star gaze gallery and many more making once stay highly enjoyable. All the above properties and their upcoming new proprieties in prime tourist locations in the state are together known as Royal Group of Hotels-for the rich and famous-which is well known in the fields of hotel, travel and tourism all over India and abroad.

Education

For Royal Group the field of education is not new. By the end of eighties before the policy of liberalization and globalization was heard, at a time when new products and technology with foreign tie ups were all poised to enter the Indian market and when there was acute shortage of trained manpower, Royal Group was quick to take initiative in establishing job oriented courses in the state. Thus was born School of Engineering. By conducting Kerala Government Engineering courses in different streams at Trivandrum over a decade, the education division of Royal Group has marked their presence in the field of Technical Education.

Catering College, with its different divisions is functioning in a multi level operating system imparting courses in Hotel Management at various levels. The college has got approval from the All India Council for Technical Education (AICTE) New Delhi and the Government of Kerala for conducting 3 year Diploma course in Hotel Management and Catering Technology at Munnar. In association with the largest educational chain in the world-the Educational Institute of American Hotel & Lodging Association (AH&LA) USA the college offers specialized courses in Front Office Management, Housekeeping Management, Principles of Food Production, Food & Beverage Service and International Hotel Management in addition to Professional Cookery at their branches at Cochin, Calicut and Trivandrum also.

As a recognition of the facilities and the reputation, the renowned Punjab Technical University has approved Munnar Catering College as their outside study centre in conducting different Hotel Management courses at Diploma, Postgraduate Diploma, Degree and Postgraduate Degree level at their Cochin and Trivandrum branches.

The educational division of the Royal Group also conducts courses in Pharmaceutical Sciences with approval from the Government of Kerala, the Pharmacy Council of India and AICTE and Para Medical Courses in association with The Punjab Technical University under Distance Education Programme. The Institute of Pharmaceutical Sciences established in the capital city of the state is now offering Diploma in Pharmacy for eligible candidate selected as per specified norms fixed for the purpose, whereas the Institute of Para Medical Sciences, Trivandrum offers courses for Diploma in Hospital Management, Diploma, P.G Diploma, B.Sc & M.Sc. degrees in Medical Laboratory Technology.

By conducting Kerala Government Engineering courses in different streams at Trivandrum over a decade, the education division of Royal Group has marked their presence in the field of Technical Education also.

On the Job Training

For developing competence in the operation of all departments of a hotel an unmatched opportunity is wide open for the students of Munnar Catering College to get trained at own hotel and resort which many other institutions cannot offer. Students of Munnar Catering College are offered on the job training in all the departments of own hotels under guidance and supervision of experienced and talented professionals exclusively appointed for the purpose. In addition to this, to get a better understanding and first hand information of what is happening around in the hospitality industry the students are also sent for practical training during their course of study to other reputed hotels too, as part of their curriculum in Hotel Management.

HOTELS AND CATERING SECTOR

This second article in the Sector Futures series on the hotels and catering sector looks at the trends and drivers affecting the sector, presents a framework to link them together and assesses their impact. The article also reviews some scenario work relating to the sector before concluding with an examination of the implications on the sector of the drivers and scenarios. Examples of the implications include better working conditions, consolidation and more consumer protection. Following the overview of the sector and initial look at trends and drivers in the first article of this series, this article now examines these trends and drivers in more detail and reviews existing foresight research on the hotels and catering sector.

Trends and Drivers of Change

The discussion above identified and introduced several trends and drivers that are shaping the sector. In a STEEP (social, technological, economic, environmental and political) breakdown, the key social drivers were identified as ageing populations and changing lifestyles and tastes. Information technologies, along with new production and kitchen technologies, were identified as the key technological drivers.

Economic drivers included globalisation and low-cost travel, which in part raise issues about skill levels, migration and competition. Regarding environmental drivers, the main issues were identified as the direct impact of climate change on the sector as part of the tourist industry and the political desire to improve energy and resource efficiency across the economy.

The key political drivers are likely to be legislation to improve consumer and worker rights, along with the quality and labelling of food. Beyond that, the sector, as part of the tourist industry, remains sensitive to the impact of international relations on consumer behaviour. The links and interactions between these forces are shown in the schematic diagram below.

STEEP Analysis

The following table summarises the STEEP factors affecting, or expected to affect, the industry along with their possible impacts.

Table 1: STEEP analysis and possible future of hotels and catering industry

Trends and drivers	Possible future of hotels and catering industry
Social	
Ageing population	Ageing consumers create a new type of demand. Older workers push harder for better conditions and better-qualified young workers choose other careers. These pressures lead to more social dialogue and an improvement in working conditions.

Contd...

Trends and drivers	Possible future of hotels and catering industry
Change in tastes and demands	More informed and flexible consumers demand more value and more personal service. Increase in niche markets, e.g. organic/ethical restaurants, health hotels, etc.; expansion of budget hotels.
Technological	
Information technologies	Leads to better resource management and more flexible service delivery. Consequently, creates demand for new IT skills and less demand for traditional skills. This may shift gender balance in the work-force.
New kitchen technology	Outsourcing and simplification of kitchen operations expected to turn kitchens into assembly lines, deskill staff and bring about lower wages. This may lead to higher margins for companies.
Internet	Expands the range of information providers and establishments on offer to consumers and leads to changes in shopping behaviour. For firms, it expands the customer base and creates new competition, raises the importance of presentation and quality of service and demands new marketing strategies.
Economic	
Low-cost air travel	More tourists and more trips taken, but expenditure patterns are unclear; expansion of services in new destinations. Long-term growth may be curbed by environmental concerns.
Globalisation	New geographic and consumer markets pose threats and opportunities to the sector. Likely to favour large enterprises and promote consolidation. Likely to stimulate debate on skill levels and migration.

Contd...

Trends and drivers	Possible future of hotels and catering industry
Environmental	
Climate change	Negative impact on the industry in affected tourist areas. Policy on use of energy resources might bring about cultural and hardware changes.
Environmental awareness`	Increased focus on dealing with pollution and waste management results in more environmentally friendly resource use, which may raise costs.
Political	
Legislation	Improvements in working conditions, consumer protection and product information increase costs for businesses. Small businesses are the most affected, because the improvements encourage consolidation. Effects filter down the supply chain and could alter the products on offer.
EU enlargement	Within the EU, increased tourist demand, migration and competition.
Social dialogue	Better industrial relations and working conditions, with higher skill levels. Potential to reduce labour turnover.

ASSESSMENT

Economic Drivers

Globalisation has affected all parties. It has pushed governments to cooperate and integrate more, and in doing so has made the world more accessible to all parties. Economically, it has reduced restrictions on the movement of capital, labour and resources. For the consumer, it has opened up new parts of the world, thus the hotels and restaurants most dependent on tourism face stiffer competition for their services, but they may also benefit from tourist visits from newly accessible regions. For companies, it opens up a larger market and offers the possibility of greater economies of scale that benefit larger chain groups and encourage consolidation. Recent trends show that many companies in the sector have chosen to expand by means of mergers or acquisitions as they become more aware of the need to pool resources in order to compete effectively in an expanding market.

The rise in low-cost air travel has above all benefited consumers, offering them more choice, flexibility and pricing options. While establishments are receiving increased numbers of visitors, it is not clear that the increase in visitor spending has been commensurate with the increase in numbers. Many tourists have become far more cost conscious, leading to a growing demand for budget, no-frills hotels. The EU market for low-cost travel still has some way to go before it reaches maturity, so the effects have probably not yet reached a plateau. However, with governments looking increasingly set to levy environmental taxes on air travel and with oil prices rising and staying high, ticket prices can be expected to rise also. The impact of this on consumer demand is uncertain, as it is not yet clear how sensitive consumers are to the pricing of budget air travel.

Environmental Drivers

In general, environmental drivers are likely to have a less immediate impact on the sector than the other drivers discussed. The most direct impact is likely to be felt by establishments that form part of the tourist industry in areas affected by climate change (coastal and ski resorts) and areas of environmental interest. However, the timeframe for such effects is likely to be further in the future than for other drivers. Although freak changes or storms may wreak havoc, the resultant damage they cause is often temporary, but the permanent damage, as from rising sea levels, is taking place as a slow, gradual process. Nevertheless, the net impact on businesses in affected areas can be expected to be negative as the features that made them attractive in the first place are eroded. While some may be able to adapt to the new environment, their success is likely to depend on how consumers react. In other respects the impact of environmental changes is likely to be felt through policies to reduce emissions, to improve the use of all resources, especially energy resources, and to reduce pollution by improving waste management.

Although much of the focus has been on power generation plants, all companies are under pressure to be more energy efficient and such pressures are likely to increase in the medium term. Furthermore, the timeframe for these drivers may be longer than for others, as environmental concerns are often low on the political agenda, and it is not easy to reach political consensus on environment-energy policies when these are believed to curb growth. Any costs created by environmental policy can be expected to affect enterprises in the first place, and it will be up to them how to deal with this. The obvious choice is to pass it on to customers, but regardless of whether this is done or not, any additional costs are likely to favour larger enterprises that enjoy greater economies of scale and have more flexibility in absorbing costs.

Political Drivers

New legislation, such as smoking bans, changes to licensing laws and new regulations governing food safety, is partly a response to changes in people's tastes and lifestyles. However, new laws can bring great costs to businesses. The smoking ban, for example, has improved conditions for workers and customers, but at the same time there is evidence that it has reduced turnover and that this has translated into job losses. Over the medium term, firms are likely to face increased demands from consumers for more informative marking and higher-quality standards for food. How governments will respond to such pressure from consumers is unclear. In the UK, for example, the quality of catered school meals became a hot topic in 2005 after the poor quality of such meals was highlighted by a high-profile chef on TV. One company supplying such meals (Compass) has suffered as a result, and the UK government is taking action to improve the quality of school meals. On the other hand, among the proposed EU laws recently scrapped by the EC president, José Barroso, there was one on food labelling. Nevertheless, governments may still be willing to take initiatives independently of EU legislation in order to satisfy their electorates.

The enlargement of the EU has positively impacted on the hotels and catering sector because the new Member States provide a new source of demand. However, migration from the new to the old Member States in pursuit of higher wages and a better standard of living is turning out to be lower than had been expected before accession. Moreover, because economic growth in the new Member States is expected to accelerate now that they are in the EU, rising wage levels and improved standards of living will probably make migration to EU15 countries less attractive.

New policies are helping to expand the scope of social dialogue within the hotels and catering sector. Social dialogue is becoming a major part of good governance because it allows all stakeholders to be part of policymaking within the firm and industry. On the other hand, union membership in this sector is comparatively low, making it difficult for workers to agree on objectives and to present a united front.

Sociological Drivers

Sociological changes, such as changes in lifestyles, are driven by and affect consumers, and directly affect businesses. The temporal impact varies, but some changes, such as the increased use of the Internet for shopping, have had a profound impact on the industry. Such drivers require businesses to adapt in order to survive, for example, by reviewing their relationship with the customer and their marketing strategy. An ageing population will affect the composition of the work-force (as outlined in the first article) and may help improve working conditions; it is also likely to lead to a change in the composition of consumer demand. In addition, growing interest from consumers in the production and health aspects of food is increasing pressure on caterers to supply better-quality food, produced in socially responsible ways, and with information on its origins. Reluctance by the industry to act on these issues is leading to increased governmental involvement. Changes to the supply chain in response to these trends are likely to be long-lasting.

Technological Drivers

Technology has been a primary driving force of change among consumers and in the sector, thereby helping to globalise it. While it creates opportunities, technology is also a major threat to small enterprises in the sector. Because of their small size, it is much harder for them to generate economies of scale and recover the cost of investment in new technologies. However, if they do not invest in new technologies, they are likely to lose out to those who have. The increasing use of technology has led to a need to retrain existing staff. Some industry bodies have argued that technology poses a threat to employment by reducing staff hours (as seen in the fall in full-time employment) and thus will exert downward pressure on wages. The initial boom in the use of information technologies appears to be slowing, and while its use will continue to increase, it is likely to be at a more gradual pace.

Scenarios for the Hotels and Catering Sector

In contrast to STEEP analysis, scenario work allows us to look beyond the familiar environment. It helps the industry to prepare for the consequences of unexpected events by asking the following questions:

- What if (X) happens?
- What would be the effects on the industry if (X) were to happen?
- What are the best ways of counteracting adverse effects?

The search for scenario work on hotels and restaurants failed to discover work related solely to hotels and restaurants. It was only as part of the tourist industry that hotels and catering received attention, and so the scenario analysis here is based primarily on foresight work related to tourism. Although hotels and restaurants are part of and rely on the tourist industry, their market is not confined just to tourists. Furthermore, the published scenario work was reactive, in that it was based on dramatic events in their immediate aftermath. It did not analyse the possible effects of hypothetical events or look at observable and more prosaic trends.

In recent years, there have been several unexpected events that have affected the hotels and catering industry, such as the 9/11 terrorist attacks, the outbreak of SARS, the foot and mouth epidemic in the UK and the bombings in Madrid and London. Such shocks have a low probability of occurrence, but their impact is high. Recently, however, such shocks have become more frequent and hence people are more inclined to believe that they will happen again. It is extremely difficult to predict these shocks, but good policies at all levels (European, national or firm) or any foresight work must not ignore their possible reoccurrence. Petersen (1997) refers to these shocks as 'wild cards'. He suggests that some shocks are imaginable, and if agents are well prepared, they could be turned into manageable events: There is a general assumption that there is nothing to do about these huge surprises. However, not all wild cards are unimaginable and by identifying wild card events that may possibly occur in the future on a proactive rather than reactive matter, these can sometimes be converted into anticipated manageable events. The chance alone of averting a future catastrophe or at least preparing strategies to handle it may be reason enough to examine wild card possibilities. If not dealt with wild cards can trigger a chain of events much worse than the initial happening. A major natural disaster can for instance cause a global epidemic, which may lead to nations closing their borders in turn leading to a collapse of the airline industry and so forth. (1997, pp. 43-47)

After September 11

One topic that scenario work could not ignore was the impact of 9/11 on the travel and tourism industry. Two major scenarios were published shortly after the attack on New York. The World Travel and Tourism Council (WTTC) estimated at that time that there were 207 million people employed worldwide in the travel and tourism economy. Its 'best guess' was that the attacks would lead to 8.8 million job losses worldwide, of which 1.2 million would be in the EU.

Within six weeks of 11 September 2001, the International Labour Organisation (ILO) published the report The social impact on the hotel and tourism sector of events subsequent to 11 September 2001 (136kb), which outlined two possible scenarios:

The Best-case Scenario

Assumptions:

- 9/11 is a one-off;
- there are no other attacks in the United States (US);
- there are no other attacks in other parts of the world.

Travel to Europe, which before the attack was showing recovery from recession, would not be badly affected. Europeans would continue to travel within the continent, while travel to the Middle East was unlikely to revive in the short term. The European tourism industry would benefit as a substitute destination choice. However, US tourists, who account for a significant part of the demand in the industry, would not return to Europe for some time. The reduction in US tourists, who are recognised as big spenders, would affect upmarket restaurants and hotels the most.

The Worst-case Scenario

Assumptions:

- there are other major terrorist attacks in the US;
- there are outbreaks of terrorism in other countries;
- the ongoing war in Afghanistan spreads to other regions.

In this scenario, the tourist demand from Asia and North America would plummet. Within Europe, the travel pattern would also change depending on the scale and location of any attacks. Domestic travel would probably benefit, with demand shifting from the location of an attack to an alternative location. In the extreme position, personal or business holidays would come to a halt. In the ILO's best-case scenario, the WTTC predictions were pessimistic. In the ILO's worst-case scenario, the consequences are far worse than the WTTC's predictions.

Iraq War Scenarios

When the US and the UK decided to invade Iraq in 2003, WTTC looked at the possible outcomes of the Iraq war and their consequences for the US tourist industry in its 2003 research on the United States-Travel and tourism, a world of opportunity (526kb, pp.18-21). The WTTC's scenario was informed by the experience of the 1991 Gulf war, the effects of which, according to the WTTC, were to limit economic growth through three main channels: higher oil prices, shattered consumer and business confidence and lower equity prices.

The base scenario: diplomatic solution or victory after a short, contained war. In the base case, the war is assumed to be short, contained and successful, and to remove global uncertainty. The effects on oil prices, confidence and equity prices are assumed to be very similar to what they would have been had there been a diplomatic solution to the crisis. In the short term, economic growth is assumed to be higher due to increased government spending. The difference in the effects on travel and tourism between no war and a speedy, contained war is therefore predicted to be small. However, the threat of war was assumed to undermine confidence and to reduce international travel, and this would affect the travel and tourism industry more than the rest of the economy.

Assumptions:

- quick, decisive victory or diplomatic solution;
- no use of weapons of mass destruction (WMD) against US troops, Israel or region;
- no reduction in OPEC oil production and exports;
- no challenges to Arab governments in region;
- new Iraqi government installed and in control;
- no damage to oil-producing capacity in Iraq or elsewhere.

The war scenario: victory with regional disruption

Under this scenario, a longer-lasting war results in persistently higher oil prices, with a deeper and longer fall in confidence and equity markets. The effects on the travel and tourism industry are expected to be more severe.

Assumptions:

- Iraq attacks oil facilities in region, with limited damage but political and economic knock-on effects;
- Iraq attacks Israel and US troops but not with WMD effective enough to trigger a major response or to have highly lethal effects;

- unexpected protracted Iraqi military resistance;
- limited Israeli intervention in war; rising political unrest in region;
- low-level civil tensions and clashes in Iraq after military conflict is over;
- some terrorist attacks on US interests.

These pressures were predicted to lead to a slowing of between 1% and 2% in GDP growth in the US and UK. The effects on the travel and tourism industry are more severe under the war scenario. In the US, under this scenario, in 2003 the travel and tourism industry would experience:

- 0.9% fall in industry demand;
- 3.7% fall in industry GDP;
- 8.9% fall in exports;
- loss of 449,100 jobs.

Climate Change Scenarios

Although the global climate has been changing for some time, there is uncertainty about its future path and patterns as well as the consequences. Research commissioned by the World Tourism Organisation (WTO) suggests two possible scenarios on global climate change, relating specifically to the tourist industry in Hungary, The responses of Lake Balaton to global cliamte change (299kb, Rátz, 2003).

Climate Zone Shift Scenario

Assumptions:

- The temperate climate zone covering Hungary shifts northward and is replaced by a warmer climate.

This would be expected to lead to a longer summer season with much higher temperatures. This could have benefits for the tourist industry, assuming the temperatures are not too high and droughts are infrequent. In contrast, winter sports tourism is likely to disappear under such a scenario.

Ice Caps Melt Scenario

Assumptions:

- Ice caps melt due to global warming.

Under this scenario, the Gulf Stream cools down and changes the climate in Europe. The Hungarian climate becomes colder and wetter. This would have a mainly negative impact on the tourism industry, as the summer season becomes shorter and wetter. However, it could lead to the further development of winter sports tourism.

Scenario Summary

Some scenario work relevant to the hotels and catering industry tends to focus on dramatic events. In some cases, the work is done after the shocks have occurred, with a best-case scenario assuming that these shocks are unique and the worst-case scenario assuming that they are not. In hindsight, it is easy to say that it is a pity such analysis was not conducted before the events occurred and that there were no plans to deal with the consequences of such events. Regarding the climate change scenario, it should be emphasised that it related to Hungary only. Furthermore, the study's primary focus was not the effect of climate change on the hotels and catering sector; instead, it formed part of a wider discussion on the overall impact of climate change on the region. Since the concern here is the European hotels and catering sector, the major drawback of the Iraq war scenario is its focus on the US tourist industry.

Moreover, to date there appears to have been little work done on exploring the future of the industry through scenario planning in the light of the various current influences identified in the first two articles of this series. It may be more useful to project these current trends and drivers and identify possible outcomes and responses.

Possible scenarios to consider are:

- What if the current weakness of the EU economy persists for much longer than expected?
- What if there is a collapse in the world financial market?
- What if there are more outbreaks of deadly viruses?
- What are the implications of developing countries becoming developed over the next 10 years?
- What would happen if the Internet ceased to exist, e.g. because of political censorship?
- What if the current skills gaps remain in 10 or 15 years' time?
- What will the role of information technologies be in the industry in the future, and how will this affect labour demand?
- What are the implications if the European Union breaks up?
- What are the implications of a Europe-wide zero immigration policy?
- What are the implications for labour supply if there are no government pensions?

Implications

As younger workers increasingly become more qualified, they are less likely to consider the hotels and catering industry, with its poorer working conditions, as a career option. This and the ageing of the population are likely to persuade businesses to employ older workers. Because of their circumstances, older workers are often less mobile and have other commitments. Consequently, they are likely to be more demanding about working conditions, to be more favourable to union membership and to become more involved in social dialogue.

Changing lifestyles and more demanding consumers are likely to promote the development of more specialised enterprises and broaden competition among hotels and restaurants. The more specialised nature of services should allow firms to charge a premium. These niche markets are likely to attract multinationals as other parts of the hotels and catering industry become commoditised and less profitable. Commoditisation exerts downward pressure on premiums and profits. In order to survive and make a profit, firms offering commoditised services can be expected to cut costs and homogenise the service/experience on offer.

On the supply side, the increasing use of technology will continue to help establishments better manage their resources and reduce spare capacity. A better knowledge of future demands has implications for staff, in that establishments are likely to seek more flexible working patterns to match demands. This in turn has implications for lifestyle and for where the savings go. On the demand side, the Internet, wireless computing and 3G mobile telephony all make it easier for consumers to obtain information, compare prices and value for money and shop around. This trend and the increasing use of the Internet as a marketing device by businesses will lead to more intense competition and make it harder to close a sale. Firms are increasingly likely to respond by seeking staff with skills in information and communication technologies (ICT), including marketing, sales and web design.

Any increase in outsourcing in the catering industry further separates the consumer from food producers, making it harder to check the origin of food. This implies a possible widening of the information gap and is likely to increase pressure on catering companies to provide information about the food they serve. Businesses can be expected to resist this because of the cost implications, so governments may intervene. The use of technology in the kitchen can be expected to raise productivity and lower labour demand. This again has implications for where the savings go. Increased productivity should see wages rise, but lower reliance on chefs' food preparation skills would have the opposite effect.

In the context of globalisation, EU enlargement offers a larger labour pool and facilitates migration.

It is unclear to what extent this will help to fill the skills gap, as the tourist industry in most new Member States is small in comparison to that in France or the UK, for example. However, as long as relative wage differentials between regions are large enough, workers in poorer regions can be expected to move to richer regions for work.

This can be expected to lower employment costs in the hotels and catering industry in richer regions. Furthermore, this is likely to attract the most skilled from the poorer regions, thus hindering the development of the industry there.

At the same time, in enlarging the EU hotel and catering market and making it more accessible, globalisation has created an opportunity for companies to exploit substantial economies of scale. To what extent this could approach the scale seen in the US, for example, is unclear given the much wider cultural and language differences that exist in the EU. Nevertheless, it is still likely to lead to the increased presence of larger multinational hotel and catering chains, which is likely to fuel the demand for migrant labour in order to reduce employment costs.

Customers may suffer if this leads to a homogenisation of service on offer, but brand names and reputations should ensure a higher-quality product.

In order to maintain this, companies can be expected to recruit the best-skilled staff and improve working conditions in order to retain them.

The skills gap in the industry adversely affects the quality of service in the industry and damages the industry's reputation among travellers. This lessens establishments' pricing power and makes it harder to attract customers. This implies handsome rewards for companies that fill the gap (with good practice putting firms on a virtuous cycle) and premium wages for those with the necessary skills.

The existence of the gap suggests that firms are unwilling to undertake training themselves and that working conditions need to be improved in order to attract and retain skilled staff. Establishments therefore have to take a more proactive and united approach.

Although low-cost airlines have increased the frequency of trips made by travellers, they often stay for a shorter duration and tend to be more cost-conscious. Furthermore, as profit-maximising companies independent of political or national influence, low-cost carriers will not hesitate to scrap unprofitable services.

This has implications for policy as well as the hotels and catering industry's marketing strategy at a local level. In some regions, the rapid growth in the tourism and leisure industry is likely to work against raising levels of education or skills, while its effect on wages will depend on the industrial structure of the locality.

Legislation to improve the working environment, e.g. smoking bans in bars and restaurants and working time regulations, has negative implications for firms' margins and labour demand. In response, firms are likely to push for productivity gains and seek more cost-effective labour and a greater application of technology.

Political concern over consumer health and the content of food is increasing pressure on catering firms to reduce sugar and salt levels, for example, in prepared food.

If catering firms respond to such concerns, this could create new demands for new tastes in food. If health problems such as diabetes and obesity become greater public health issues, then the prospect of health-related taxes on food must surely draw closer. Growing concern among consumers about the origin of their food and the production methods involved is largely a social trend, but it, too, is generating political pressure for more information and increased food labelling.

This raises the prospect of legislation forcing the industry to inform consumers. The disclosure of more information and the demand for food produced in more socially responsible ways is likely to promote good practice in the food supply chain, and may lead to a shift away from low-end food establishments.

In the wake of the 9/11 attacks, the EU hotels and catering sector saw turnover growth slow dramatically. US visitor numbers to the EU are only now returning to the pre-9/11 levels. International relations remain fractured because of the US-led 'war on terror' and the Iraq war.

The continuation of political and military hostilities and the continued involvement of EU nations mean that some EU Member States remain targets for terrorism, as seen in the Madrid and London bombings. US tourist confidence is therefore likely to remain fragile.

High-profile marketing campaigns may be needed in the US to bolster confidence. That US visitor levels are recovering suggests terrorism has not inflicted long-lasting damage on the industry. Such damage could be caused, however, if one location were to suffer multiple attacks within a space of two or three years.

While the industry is likely to be able to recover from this on an EU level, the impact on the affected region is likely to last longer. Heavy discounting in response, as employed in London in recent years, whether successful or not, would probably lead to lower levels of employment and investment, and a deterioration in working conditions. Such a downward spiral would take years to reverse.

SUMMARY

This concludes the review of the key trends and drivers affecting the sector, and of scenario work relating to the sector. The reader should have a better idea of what issues are driving the sector and of the paucity of scenario work relating to the sector.

Having looked at the trends and scenarios and their implications, the third and last article in this series, Hotels and catering-policies, issues and the future, carries the discussion forward to look at major policy issues and challenges facing the sector. Consideration is given to their timeframe and the agents and regions affected.

14

Revenue Management

MEANING

When you stayed in that luxury hotel during your last vacation, did you check what your neighbour paid for her room? If she were a business visitor, she could have paid well above $300 for the same room that you paid $180. It is also possible that she paid $120 provided she planned well in advance and managed to get that "better" deal which was elusive to you. So why do hotels charge different customers different rates for the same type of room? Such differences are the result of an increasingly common strategy to maximize revenue (and profits) in the Hotel industry–a practice referred to as Revenue or Yield Management.

Revenue Management (RM) is a scientific technique that combines Operations Research, Statistics and Customer Relationship Management (CRM) and categorizes customers into price bands, based on various services. Statistical analysis of past data helps in forecasting demand and establishing the appropriate price bands. Applied correctly, Revenue Management helps hotels expand market size and increase revenues. Some industry practitioners also refer to RM as the art of selling the right room to the right customer at the right time and for the right price.

To understand the need for an RM system, let us take the following two examples. At the peak of the SARS epidemic in Canada, a resort experienced a 25% drop in number of visitors. Amazingly, this resort managed to limit decline in revenue to a bare 3%. During economic depression, a travel management company reduced its marketing budget by half, but still managed a revenue increase of 6%. How were these successes possible? The answer to both of these questions lies with the implementation of Revenue Management strategy.

NEED OF REVENUE MANAGEMENT?

- *Segmented Market:* Hotels typically segment their market (customer base) into a set of categories based on the price each category is willing to pay. Typical categories include the business traveler and the vacation traveler. Because demand patterns for each of these categories may vary significantly, hotels find it difficult to satisfy all of the demand simultaneously. A good example is the comparison between the time-conscious business executive and the price-sensitive vacation customer. The former is willing to pay a higher price in exchange for flexibility of being able to book a room at the last minute while the latter is willing to give up some flexibility for the sake of a more inexpensive room. RM tries to maximize revenues by managing the trade-off between a low occupancy and higher room rate scenario (business customers) versus a high occupancy and lower room rate (vacation customers). Such a strategy allows hotels to fill rooms that would otherwise have been empty.
- *Fixed Capacity*: A hotel's capacity is relatively fixed-it is nearly impossible to add or remove rooms based on fluctuations in demand. If at all hotel capacity were flexible, there would be no need to manage capacity.
- *Perishable Inventory*: In the hotel industry, hotel rooms are the inventory. A hotel room that remains

unoccupied for a night loses all its value for that night. This inventory cannot be stored and is lost forever. Because RM tries to manage demand instead of supply, it proves to be good business sense for the hotel.

- *Low Marginal Cost*: The fixed cost of adding a room in a hotel is heavily capital intensive. However, once the hotel manages to cover its initial fixed costs, the cost of serving an additional customer is low enough that the hotel can sell the room at a lower margin if it wishes. Such a strategy will obviously need to be balanced by one that also seeks to sell the room(s) at higher margins. Thus, the high fixed cost/low marginal cost nature of the business makes price differentiation a necessity-something that is made possible by application of RM.
- *Advanced Sales*: More often than not, requests for bookings start early. Therefore, hotels have enough leeway to adjust room prices based on the variation between realized bookings and expected demand. If all hotel rooms are sold at the same time, the hotel does not have the flexibility to adjust prices upward if demand picks up later. The trade-off occurs when a manager is faced with the option of accepting an early reservation from a customer who wants a low price, or waiting to see if a higher paying customer will eventually show up...
- *Demand Fluctuations*: Demand for hotel rooms is characterized by crests and troughs, which the hotel factors in during the room pricing process. In peak season, the hotel can increase its revenues by raising room prices, while during lean seasons it can increase its utilization rate by lowering prices. Past data will offer the manager a way to forecast when these periods of high and low demand may occur. Unfortunately, it is very difficult to predict the actual demand with a high degree of certainty.

Therefore, the most critical challenge facing the hotel industry is predicting potential capacity, and developing a pricing strategy that will encourage maximum capacity and revenue. Revenue Management is the most effective technique to solve this challenge, similar to aggregate and hierarchical production planning techniques often employed in the manufacturing industry.

Revenue Management is based on complex optimization methodologies developed from advanced statistical and analytical models. In order to arrive at a solution, managers need to evaluate several millions of decisions, which requires a significant investment of skills, hardware and time. Many RM practitioners prefer to breakdown the actual business scenario into four sub-problems, and then identify an individual solution to some or all of these sub-problems. This would significantly reduce the number of potential non-optimal decisions thereby providing fewer choices, leading to quicker results.

These four sub-problems are:

(a) Market segment identification,

(b) Forecasting and Pricing,

(c) Inventory allocation, and

(d) Overbooking.

Working

Market Segment Identification: The first and foremost step in a hotel RM system is the identification of the various market segments for the hotel room, followed by implementation of a differential pricing scheme. The objective in front of the hotel is the expansion of its market and in motivating the customer to pay more than he/she will usually spend. It is further observed that customers in the business class segment are less sensitive to higher prices as opposed to those in the vacation segment. An RM system helps hotels create additional price-points by building physical and logical fences around the different market segments, as shown in the table below.

CHARACTERISTICS	HIGHER PRICE	LOWER PRICE
Physical Fences		
View	Pool view, ocean view, hill view	Non-scenic view
Size	Bigger room with more facilities and gadgets	Smaller rooms with fewer facilities
Temporal	Weekday bookings	Weekend bookings
Logical Fences		
Length of Stay	Short stay. Often one or two days	Longer stay. One night revenue can spoil three nights revenue when demand is high
Flexibility	Cancellations and rescheduling are allowed at a low penalty	High penalty for cancellation and schedule changes
Time of Purchase	Bookings are made very close to date of check-in	Bookings are made quite early
Privileges	Are rewarded loyalty privileges either as free services or free stay vouchers	No privileges
Size of Business Provided	Corporate business customers booking frequently	Self funding vacationers booking rarely
Point of Sale	Physical delivery and confirmations	By email or phone

Demand Forecasting: The next step in an RM process is forecasting demand and pricing of the different market segments. Pricing and demand are inter-related and need to be coordinated. In the hotel industry, demand for a room is cyclic in nature (day of a week, months of a year) and follows a trend (demand growth due to economic growth). These forecasts are seldom precise but provide the decision-maker with an approximate set of inputs that are used in the planning process. RM models help pinpoint demand by minimizing uncertainty and producing the best possible forecast.

Allocation: The next important step in a RM process is the allocation of inventory (hotel rooms) among different market segments. The ratio of discounted versus full priced rooms is not fixed during the reservation period; rather, it is "tweaked" appropriately as the date of stay approaches. The opportunity cost of selling a discounted room instead of a full priced one has to be measured in order to make the best decision. Thus, when a customer approaches the hotel for a discounted price, the manager needs to evaluate this scenario with the expected revenue from another customer who might come at a later date, willing to pay a higher price for the same room. The manager would accept the request only if the discounted price now is more than the expected price at which the room might be booked by the second customer. The key word here is "expected". RM systems use complicated mathematical algorithms to arrive at this decision using techniques such as Littlewoods and Expectation Maximization, referred to as the EM algorithm.

To explain these techniques, let us consider a simple two class scenario. A hotel has two price categories of rooms, say $60 and $100. Since the pricing is different for the two rooms, these rooms are each targeted at a different customer set. Based on the historical preference pattern of customers in each segment, it would be possible to estimate the number of customers who would be willing to buy these rooms at the given price, with a reasonable "variance". The term variance refers to a tolerance level. For example, an average 50 customers may be willing to pay $100 for some rooms, but it could also mean that the actual number of customers who turn up for the $100 room could be 60 (or even 40) with some probability, or 80 (or 30) with a lesser probability. In statistical terms, this sort of pattern for the different customer segments is said to mimic a normal distribution.

Using the past data and applying statistical know-how, we can actually estimate an "expectation" of revenue by quantifying the probability of a specific demand value and the actual revenue. In the same example, let us assume that this hotel has 100 rooms, which are similar, but priced at the time of booking. If the booking is done fairly closely to the actual date of stay, the customers may need to pay $100, whereas, they might have paid only $60 had they booked in advance. Remember that, on an average, 50 persons are willing to pay $100 for this room. Obviously, many more than 50 (say, 120) are willing to $60 for the same room. We can use the Littlewoods rule to actually estimate the number of rooms that must be protected for those customers who are willing to pay $100. If we protect too many rooms, some rooms may go vacant thereby resulting in a loss of potential revenue of at least $60 per room. On the other hand if we protect too few rooms for $100 customers, we lose the opportunity of $40 per room on that number of rooms. The Littlewoods rule guides us to arrive at an optimal number of rooms that would maximize the expectation of revenues.

Overbooking: Overbooking is the practice of intentionally selling more rooms than are available in order to offset the effect of cancellations and no-shows. Studies estimate that although a hotel is fully booked, about 5-8% of the rooms are vacant on any given date. Poor overbooking decisions can prove to be very expensive for the hotel. In the short run, it is only a loss of room revenue, but over the long-term, casualties may include decreased customer loyalty, loss of hotel reputation, etc. American Airlines developed an optimization model that maximizes net revenues associated with overbooking decisions for the airline industry.

To illustrate the overbooking model developed by the American Airlines, let us consider a B757 jet flying from Chicago to Boston. The aircraft has about 180 seats. Based on the past travel pattern, it is observed that an average of 5% (or nine passengers) do not turn up at the time of boarding the flight. If the airlines book all seats for this leg, it is likely to fly with only 171 occupied seats. However it does not mean that it never flies with 172 or more (even 180) seats occupied. There is a lesser chance of the flight flying with 172 passengers, an even lesser chance of it flying with 175 and a miniscule chance of it flying with all 180 passengers. Therefore, if we book 181 passengers instead of 180, we are likely to end up with only 173 passengers (and almost always with lesser than 180 passengers). In an odd event of exactly 181 passengers reporting, the airline would need to bump one passenger. IATA has defined rules to compensate bumped passengers. If we can quantify all costs (including the cost of lost goodwill), the expected revenue would be the revenue from 181 passengers minus the expected cost of compensating the one additional passenger at that odd chance. Since the probability of exactly 181 passengers turning up is so low, the revenue from that additional passenger generally compensates more than the expected cost. For this example, the optimal number of passengers that can be booked would be 186 as illustrated in the figure below.

This model can be directly applied to the hotel industry as well. The driving force behind the model is the evaluation of the trade-off between additional revenue accrued by selling an already-reserved room versus the downside from doing so. It has been found that net revenue increases with overbooking until the point where the downside from overbooking a room exceeds customer revenues. Beyond that point, the negative impact of overbooking increases rapidly because fewer and fewer customers appreciate being turned away.

CHALLENGES

It is quite clear that while an RM system can guarantee increased revenues, it can be quite complicated to design and requires high levels of expertise for implementation. Some of the challenges facing hotels in the implementation of a robust and accurate RM system include:

- Measuring performance of an RM system is a major issue. Occupancy rates and yield are measures that are affected by external competition. An ideal measurement can be done using an opportunity model that indicates where the hotel stands in comparison to its maximum and
- Differential pricing is here to stay-customers seem resigned to the fact that hotels charge different prices for the same room. However, some customers do not like this practice and penalize the hotel by not becoming a patron. Therefore, in a fiercely competitive

environment where quality of service is the key to success, RM may not work. In evaluating the efficiency of a RM system, the trade-off between generating short-term profits and creating long-term customer loyalty and "mindshare" needs to be studied carefully.

- From an operational point of view, RM can impact the motivational level of the employees. In many cases, RM takes much of the guess work out of employees, thereby reducing their decision-making responsibilities. Sometimes, employees taking reservations are paid a percentage of the sales they make, motivating them to make group bookings, which in turn may be contradictory with the objectives of an RM system.

SUMMARY

As part of ongoing changes in the industry, companies throughout the entire hospitality spectrum are placing a strong emphasis on implementing major operational changes. Beyond recognizing that meaningful cost reductions must be achieved without compromising safety, capacity and service levels, they are also looking at reducing costs by increasing flexibility and improving asset utilization through an RM strategy. In doing so, they continue to reassess their true core competencies, and are looking to outsource many of these processes, as they look to optimize business efficiencies and increase profitability.

15

Assisted Living: New Opportunities for Hospitality

INTRODUCTION

As the baby boom becomes an elder boom in coming decades, profound change will occur across North America and Europe as the elderly become a dominant part of the population. In the United States, 80 million babyboomers began to turn 50 in the last year and many are already looking to early retirement. Almost half of Europe's population could be over 60 by the year 2050 as population growth slows. Those approaching retirement age today are at the vanguard of this much heralded demographic change, and with it, radical change in society's structure and business opportunity. Among those sectors expected to accelerate in demand is the assisted living marketplace.

Assisted living represents a middle ground for the elderly. Housing accompanied by some assistance allows seniors to remain independent as long as possible. Services are tailored to the individual as they need them. Meanwhile, Wall Street has eagerly embraced offerings made by leaders in the industry, recognizing the significant growth prospects for assisted living. This $16.5 billion market is projected to exceed $20 billion in revenues by the year 2000 in the United States alone. Assisted living represents a prime opportunity for hospitality companies willing to use the core competencies of hospitality to develop and operate communities for seniors.

While most of the major hospitality entities have merged, consolidated or entered new market segments in last few years only one hospitality company is currently a major player in the assisted living industry, Marriott International, which expanded into assisted living in 1989, now occupies the number two position on the chart for the top 25 U.S. Senior housing Owners and is ranked third in the top 25 U.S. Senior Housing Managers. In June of 1996, Marriott completed its merger with Forum Group, in the process acquiring an additional 42 assisted living facilities. As of October 1997, Marriott operated 82 assisted living communities, and the company plans to triple that number in the next five years.

Does Marriott's path in assisted living make sense for other hospitality companies? Clearly there are "cross-over" resources and skills between the hospitality and assisted living industries. Food and beverage and other processes in hospitality can be translated into assisted living operations. Indeed, hospitality companies with brands that represent service and quality have two of the most import ant ingredients when consumers make buying decisions in this industry. There are also challenges for a hospitality company expanding in this industry, however, given its mission of providing care services to the elderly. Nevertheless, the prospects may be attractive to hospitality companies with significant resources, given that assisted living is likely to be the fastest-growing segment in the long-term care industry.

TRENDS DRIVING ASSISTED LIVING

Three primary demographic trends will shape growth of the assisted living industry in the next few decades. Advances in nutrition and medical science have resulted in an increased life expectancy, and consequently growing numbers of elderly people. Many seniors are living longer, more active lives.

Second, as an increasing number of women enter the work-force, their ability to serve as the primary caregiver to aging parents has been greatly reduced, thus changing the role of the family in providing elderly care. Third, a greater number of elderly are now living in isolation in many countries. In the United States, for example, the average family moves once every five years. Many families are widely scattered, leaving elderly parents alone. Family structures have radically changed in recent decades. The end result is an elderly population that has been left without the traditional sources of assistance needed to perform their daily activities. Families must increasingly rely on alternative solutions to fulfil their previous roles as caregivers.

Proactive companies in the assisted living industry have stepped in to provide these services to a market that is forecast to grow at a record pace. The number of people aged 65 and over in the United States is currently 34 million, accounting for 13 percent of the total population. That number is projected to grow to 69 million, or 20 percent of the total population, by the year 2030.[4] The number of elderly will only increase with the aging of the baby boom generation, those individuals born between 1946 and 1964. As this generation ages and retires, an increasing number of people over the age of 75 will require some level of care or assistance during the final years of their lives. The number of people aged 85 and over is currently 3.7 million and is projected to increase to 8.5 million by the year 2030. Demand will be driven by increases in how long people live. The average life expectancy for women aged 65 is projected to increase from 84.2 years in 1995 to 87.4 years in the year 2050.

The demographic shift in the European Union (EU) may be even more extreme than in North America, where the demographic structure of society is more greatly influenced by immigration and slightly higher birth rates. The population aged 60 or over in the European Union had climbed by 50 percent in recent years, reaching 68.6 million by 1992. Estimates place the number of older people in the European Union at 80 to 100 million by the year 2020, of which 27 to

29 million are estimated to be over 80 years old. The average life expectancy in Europe is estimated at 78 years for men and 82.5 years for women. This is reported slightly lower in the United Kingdom at 77.6 years for men and 81.7 years for women.

Also of urgent concern is the financial strength of the aging in the European Union, with poverty remaining a source of worry for many older people in EU countries. A 1993 Eurostate survey revealed that 48 percent of older people in the then 12 EU countries had financial difficulties. Health and social services or older people vary widely across Europe. Generally, however, the trend is toward de-emphasizing institutionalization and promoting private care or assistance.

Although needs and resources vary greatly among the elderly in North America and Europe, assisted living will almost certainly sustain significant growth in the near future for a variety of reasons:

- Increased life expectancy of population as a whole, and of the assisted living target market;
- Decreased need for acute care by elderly;
- Increased relative wealth of elderly population;
- Decreased role of traditional substitutes to assisted living, particularly hospitals and nursing homes, as a result of cost pressures;
- Increased awareness and acceptance of assisted living services as an alternative to family care;
- Decreased lime available to traditional care providers, principally family members, creating the need for alternatives.

ASSISTED LIVING - HOW DOES IT WORK

Inspired by the Dutch and Scandinavian systems, assisted living programs originally offered housing and sheltered services for the frail elderly. Today, the industry provides long-term care in a homelike environment at less expensive rates than nursing homes. Elderly residents gain an ability to live a more autonomous lifestyle, while enjoying the comfort and security of on-site services, including health programs and other types of support. As residents age, their level of need increases, and the community becomes responsible for providing more complex levels of care. This is commonly referred to as "aging in place." Residents are able to customize their level of care based upon their needs.

A Merrill Lynch industry report indicates that the average assisted living community comprises 58 separate private living units. A typical resident is a widowed or single female, 84 years of age, who needs assistance with three activities of daily living. Some 30 to 40 percent of residents suffer from Alzheimer's or some other form of dementia.

Due to the focus on lower acuity care, assisted living communities can offer the elderly the level of care that is individually required at prices that are typically two-thirds of what a nursing home would charge. Most assisted living communities in the United States offer a tiered pricing schedule in which residents pay a basic rate for room and board, and are then charged additional fees depending on the level of service they select. This economic structure is beneficial for both the provider and the customer. The customer is able to obtain an individualized level of service at prices substantially less than at other higher acuity centers, like nursing homes. The provider is able to continuously serve customers as their needs change.

Assisted living companies in the United States are currently able to offer affordable services to their residents with monthly costs for assisted living (housing, meals and additional services) ranging from \$1,500 - \$3,000,[9] with certain markets ranging as high as \$6,000 - \$7,000. Private payers represent 96 percent of the industry's total revenue. Costs to residents could increase substantially, however, depending on the extent of future regulation. While U.S. nursing homes and other healthcare providers are heavily regulated on a federal level currently, the American assisted living industry is free of many of the costly compliance burdens of federal regulation. Regulation of the assisted living industry, however, looms on the horizon as the expansion of this industry has stimulated greater scrutiny of assisted living providers.

OPPORTUNITIES FOR HOSPITALITY

The assisted living industry is highly fragmented, with a growing trend toward consolidation. The supply of communities has been unable to keep pace with demand and consolidations have begun to accelerate. The top 50 operators in the industry housed an estimated 20 percent of the residents in 1996 until their needs required that they move to nursing homes or other higher acuity programs. Providers look to gain critical mass and strengthen their presence in particular geographic regions. This environment will create opportunities for strong operators and developers with loyal employees, an established marketing process, and access to capital.

THE COMPETITIVE LANDSCAPE

Competition among companies in the assisted living industry exists on three levels - national, regional and local. To effectively compete on a national level, a company may need to have a strong brand name, access to sufficient capital and an ability to effectively execute appropriate development decisions. On a regional level, a company will need to take advantage of regional demographics, maximize efficient use of resources and establish brand equity. On a local level, competition varies widely. Factors influencing the local markets include geographic location, knowledge of the elderly population trends currently and going forward, and regulatory issues. Also critical are supply-and-demand forces shaping the local market in its current phase and what is expected for the future.

MARKETING TO CUSTOMERS

To effectively position companies within key markets, it is essential to understand the distinction between the prospective resident of the assisted living community and the customer who may be an adult child caring for an aging parent. In the assisted living industry, there are unique challenges to target and market to the consumer (the potential resident of the assisted living facility). The customer, however, may be the adult child who is the primary caregiver. Most residents - or their family caregivers - choose an assisted living community within a certain radius of their family. This highlights the importance of careful target marketing to identify not only the demographics of the resident, but also of the family.

ACCESS TO CAPITAL

As competition continues to increase, access to capital will be a major factor in success. Currently, the ability to obtain capital in the public and private markets in the United States is at an unprecedented level as investors recognize the opportunities and returns of the assisting living market. Within The last 24 months, there have been 16 public equity offerings, six convertible offerings and multiple REIT financings by assisted living companies in the United States. In a capital-constrained environment, those companies with access to capital through relationships with strategic partners will have a competitive advantage. Again, strong hospitality entities would be able to supplement local assisted living operators.

COMPETITIVE AND MARKET CONCLUSIONS

The fundamentals driving the assisted living industry - including the aging of populations in advanced economies and the drive to better manage health care costs - will continue to provide exceptional demand for assisted living services. Given the industry's fundamentals, a company with access to capital, strategic focus and commitment to operational excellence should be well positioned to be a leader in the market. As competition in this evolving market increases, consolidation will provide companies with an opportunity to expand both within their own niche of service and into other levels of the care continuum. This is particularly the case in the United States, for example, where there is currently no dominant provider of assisted living services.

Although hospitality companies may have the brand equity and the operational expertise of running a housing community, it is essential for them to provide the other health - and support - related services to elderly residents. Residents of assisted living communities require more services than a hotel guest. That is the core difference between hospitality and assisted living. Competitors for elderly residents offer communities and services at all points of the senior care continuum, from skilled nursing communities and acute care hospitals, to companies providing home-based health care. Hospitality companies considering the assisted living market may want to consider partnerships with current operators. The hospitality companies can offer critical mass, brand reputation and general operational expertise, while the care-giving expertise would be provided by the assisted living company.

The prospects for providers of assisted living housing look extremely promising. The number of potential customers is rapidly rising, and they can be expected to have lengthy stays at assisted living communities. At the same time, there is currently a limited supply of assisted living communities. This all translates into opportunities for proactive companies. The hospitality industry may be one of the beneficiaries.

Bibliography

Auguste, E.: *Escoffier Cook Book: A Guide to the Fine Art Cookery*, New York, Crown, 1969.

Bryson, McDowell: *Concierge: Key to Hospitality: A Training Manual*, New York, Wiley, 1992.

Charles, G.: *International Dictionary of Food & Cooking*, Chicago, Fitzroy Dearborn, 1998.

Clark, Mona: *Interpersonal Skills for Hospitality Managers*, London, Chapman Hill, 1995.

Cracknell, H. L.: *Escoffier: The Complete Guide to the Art of Modern Cookery*, New York, John Wiley, 1979.

Donald, M.: *Customer Service in the Hospitality and Tourism Industry*, Englewood Cliffs, Prentice Hall, 1994.

Elio, C.: *The Hospitality Law Desk Reference*, Miami, Southern Beverage Journal, 1994.

Gisslen, Wayne: *Professional Cooking*, New York, Wiley, 1999.

Hubert, B.: *A Host of Opportunities: An Introduction to Hospitality Management*, Chicago, Irwin, 1996.

Jarvis, R.: *Business Accounting for Hospitality and Tourism*, London, Chapman and Hall, 1995.

Judi, Radice: *Restaurant & Food Graphics*, Glen Cove, PBC International, 1994.

Marjorie, E.: *Careers in Travel, Tourism, and Hospitality*, Lincolnwood, VGM Career Horizons, 1997.

Michael, John: *Principles of Hospitality Law*, London, Cassell, 1999.

Nancy, N.: *Choosing a Career in Hotels, Motels, and Resorts*, New York, Rosen Pub. Group, 1997.

Norman, G.: *Hotel, Restaurant, and Travel Law: A Preventive Approach*, Albany, Delmar Publishers, 1993.

Robert, C.: *Cases in Hospitality Marketing and Management*, New York, John Wiley, 1997.

Rocco, M.: *An Introduction to Hospitality Today*, Orlando, Educational Institute, 1998.

Rosemary, E.: *Managing Employee Relations in the Hotel and Catering Industry*, London, Cassell, 1995.

Rosenzweig, J. E.: *Organisation and Management*, New York, McGraw Hill International, 1963.

Sherman, Barry: *Telecommunications Management*, New York, McGraw Hill, 1995.

Thomas, F.: *Introduction to Management in the Hospitality Industry*, New York, Wiley, 1995.

Timothy, R.: *Cases in Hospitality Management: A Critical Incident Approach*, New York, Wiley, 1995.

Vallette, J.: *The International Trade in Wastes: A Greenpeace Inventory*, Washington, Greenpeace, 1989.

Walden, Richard: *Genetic Transformation in Plants*, England, Open University Press, 1988.

Waller, Keith: *Improving Food and Beverage Performance*, Oxford, Butterworth-Heinemann, 1996.

Ware, Richard: *How to Open Your Own Restaurant: A Guide for Entrepreneurs*, New York, Penguin Books, 1991.

Wendy, B.: *Elegant Hotels of Europe*, Glen Cove, PBC International, 1994.

William, H.: *The Chef's Guide to Practical Restaurant Cookery*, New York, Van Nostrand Reinhold, 1988.

Zupan, J.M.: *The Distribution of Air Quality in the New York Region*, Baltimore, Johns Hopkins University Press, 1973.

Index

E

F

G

H

I

OOO